Contents

INTRODUCTION

Everton Football Club rank among the most famous names in the World Game. The Goodison Park club have been one of the most consistent members of English league football and this year proudly celebrate their centenary in the top flight of English football.

The players that have starred for the Blues include some of the greatest to have graced the British game: Alex Young, Gary Lineker and Howard Kendall to name but a few.

From Harry Catterick's School of Science to Kendall's memorable team of the mid-80s, the Blues have frequently challenged for honours and have added a European Cup Winners' Cup, 4 League Titles and 3 FA Cups to their impressive pre-war trophy haul.

However as this book celebrates the contributions made to the club's success since the war by the 50 greatest players to have worn the blue shirts, any such compilation is bound to be subjective. How could one compare a player of the 1940s and 1950s, when at times Everton were in the Second Division, with the standards of the top flight today? Football has changed dramatically, particularly with the influx of overseas players and the growth of the professional game.

Though the book offers a fascinating insight into the range of footballers who have played at Goodison there is no place for the likes of Derek Mountfield or Mike Trebilcock. Therefore, I am sure the book will stimulate debate and argument over the selections made.

Dean P Hayes
Pembrokeshire
June 2003

JOHN BAILEY

Born	1 April 1957
Birthplace	Liverpool
Height	5ft 8ins
Weight	11st 8lbs

Team	Apps	Gls
Blackburn R	115 (5)	1
Everton	171	3
Newvcastle U	39 (1)	0
Bristol City	79 (1)	1

A local lad with a typically cutting sense of humour, John Bailey began his career with Blackburn Rovers where his impressive displays at left-back prompted former Ewood boss Gordon Lee to pay £300,000 for his services in July 1979. An ever-present in his first season at Goodison, Bailey soon forced his way on to the international scene being called up for England 'B' duty.

Though he was a more than capable tackler, Bailey was at his best when using his speed and control to push forward deep into enemy territory. An accurate passer of the ball, he was especially adept at hitting low crosses into the six-yard box. After playing an important role in the Blues' rise from their desperate form at the turn of the decade, it was fitting that Bailey, who was at his uplifting best in the 1984 League Cup Final draw against Liverpool, should gain compensation for

"Bailey was at his best when using his speed and control to push forward deep into enemy territory"

the 1-0 replay defeat by sharing in the team's success at the end of that season in the FA Cup triumph over Watford.

The following season his progress was hampered by a series of niggling injuries and the signing of Welsh international defender Pat Van Den Hauwe from Birmingham City. However, he played enough games to win a title medal and throughout the campaign, whether in or out of the side, he was still very much the joker in Everton's pack. Bailey liked nothing better than to wind up the club's Welsh internationals Kevin Ratcliffe and Neville Southall, delighting in informing them that his one appearance for England 'B' was worth at least fifty of their full international caps. And manager Howard Kendall wasn't immune from the practical jokes when a kissogram girl arrived at the team's hotel.

Towards the end of that 1984-85

League Championship-winning season, Bailey had a clear-the-air meeting with Kendall and was placed on the transfer list. However, within a month he had changed his mind and signed a new one-year deal. Though the Blues progressed to greater glory, Bailey, who the Everton fans loved for his total emotional commitment, joined Newcastle United for £80,000 in October 1985. He had one good season on Tyneside before losing his place to local lad Kenny Wharton. Bristol City manager Joe Jordan signed Bailey on a free transfer in September 1988 and he became an influential figure as the Robins reached the Littlewoods Cup semi-finals that season. His sole goal in exactly 100 League and Cup appearances for City clinched a 1-0 win over Crewe Alexandra in October 1989.

At the end of his career Bailey, (a useful boxer who once competed in the ABA Championships) had a brief spell on the Ashton Gate club's coaching staff. In 1992 Bailey rejoined Everton

as the club's youth coach but within a year he had lost his job. He later joined Sheffield United as assistant manager to former Blues' boss Howard Kendall.

Honours:
League Championship 1984-85
FA Cup 1983-84

ALAN BALL

Born	12 May 1945
Birthplace	Farnworth
Height	5ft 7ins
Weight	10st 0lbs

Team	Apps	Gls
Blackpool	146	46
Everton	208	56
Arsenal	177	45
Southampton	195	11
Bristol R	17	2

Football mad as a boy, Alan Ball had trials with Wolves and Bolton but was rejected by both. In the end, it was only the persistence of his footballing father Alan Ball senior that persuaded Blackpool to sign him, after Ball junior had gone to Bloomfield Road and offered to play in a trial.

Ball made his League debut for the Seasiders against Liverpool at Anfield in 1962 at the age of 17. Within twelve months he had become a regular in the Blackpool side. When Ball first joined Blackpool, Stanley Matthews, then aged 46, had the young midfielder removed from a practice match because instead of passing to Matthews' feet, he was hitting passes he expected Stanley to run on to!

Perhaps his only failing, especially in those early days, was his explosive temper, which was usually the result of a burning desire to win. His competitiveness even shone though when he was signing autographs. he would often give himself letters after his name, Alan J Ball WIN!

After making his England debut against Yugoslavia in 1965, Ball went on to star the following year in the World Cup Finals. Without a doubt, his best match was the final itself - his tirelessness, especially during extra-time, has become legendary and he set up the third and decisive goal for Geoff Hurst. The sight of him running with his socks round his ankles during the World Cup Final endeared him to the British public.

Around the time of the World Cup, Bally thought his career and game were standing still and was ambitious for a move. When it became clear he was available, there was a lot of interest, especially from Leeds United and Spurs and even from Italy. But in the end, Everton moved fast and on 15 August 1966, manager Harry Catterick signed him for £110,000.

Ball made his Everton debut at Fulham on the opening day of the

1966-67 season, scoring the game's only goal. He was the club's leading scorer in his first two seasons with the Blues and in 1967-68, when he scored 20 League goals, he netted four in the 6-2 win at West Bromwich Albion.

Playing alongside Colin Harvey and Howard Kendall in the Everton midfield, he was instrumental in the club winning the League Championship in 1969-70. Ball continued to shine for both club and country, being England's best player in the 1970 World Cup Finals when they tried to defend their title.

Always a firm favourite at Everton, Ball joined Arsenal in December 1971 for a record £220,000, manager Harry Catterick reasoning that Bally had gone stale trying to rally a flagging Everton side. After a successful career at Highbury, he moved to Southampton where he made over 200 first team appearances in two spells. History proves that the departure of Ball signalled the end of a great Everton team - he was irreplaceable as English football was no longer producing his blend of ball player. On his 67th international appearance for England, the then manager Don Revie made him captain, but five games later he was dropped after breaking a curfew. When he left the Dell, he had a short spell in Hong Kong, later resuming his playing career with Bristol Rovers.

On entering management, Ball took Portsmouth into the First Division before having mixed results in charge of Stoke City, Exeter City, Southampton and Manchester City, eventually returning to Fratton Park for a second spell in charge.

> **Honours**
> **League Championship 1969-70**
> **72 England caps**

PETER BEARDSLEY

Born	18 January 1961
Birthplace	Newcastle
Height	5ft 8ins
Weight	11st 7lbs

Team	Apps	Gls
Carlisle Utd	93 (11)	22
Newcastle U	272 (4)	108
Liverpool	120 (11)	46
Everton	81	25
Bolton W	14 (3)	2
Man City (L)	5 (1)	0
Fulham	19 (2)	4
Hartlepool U	22	2

This quick-thinking, skilful striker began his Football League career with Carlisle United after the Cumbrian club picked him up as an 18-year-old from Wallsend Boys' Club in his native Tyneside. He spent three years at Brunton Park before trying his luck in North America with Vancouver Whitecaps. Beardsley's success in the States alerted Manchester United and they brought him back to these shores but within six months he was back in Vancouver. A year later, Newcastle United manager Arthur Cox signed him as a strike partner for Kevin Keegan and in 1983-84, his first season with the club, he scored 20 League goals as the Magpies won promotion to the First Division. Following Keegan's retirement, Beardsley was Newcastle's leading scorer in the next two First Division campaigns.

While at St James' Park, Beardsley won his first international cap, coming on as a substitute in the match against Egypt in Cairo in January 1986. A late and unexpected inclusion for England's World Cup squad for the finals in Mexico led to the inspired partnership with Gary Lineker that revived a flagging campaign.

In the summer of 1987 Beardsley was surprisingly allowed to leave Newcastle for Liverpool. Along with John Barnes, he inspired another golden era for the Reds, winning a League Championship medal in his first season at Anfield. This was followed by an FA Cup winners medal in 1989 and another League title triumph the following season. As much a creator as scorer, Beardsley was never prolific for Liverpool until 1990-91 when he netted eleven goals in the first eleven games, including a hat-trick against Manchester United. Unfortunately, he then lost his place through injury but even when fully fit, he was ignored by manager Kenny Dalglish. Although he was restored to first team duty after Dalglish's dramatic departure, it still

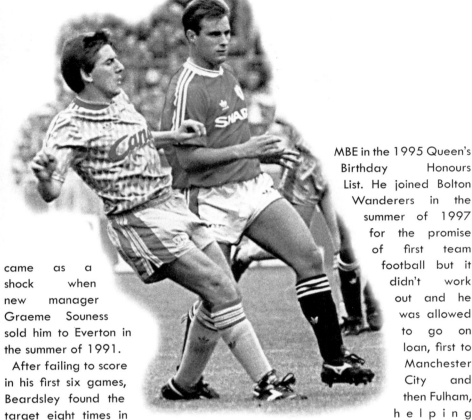

came as a shock when new manager Graeme Souness sold him to Everton in the summer of 1991.

After failing to score in his first six games, Beardsley found the target eight times in his next six outings for the Toffees and ended the season as the club's leading scorer with 19 League and Cup goals. He was the mainstay of the Everton side in two disappointing seasons, his immense skill providing some relief from the doom and gloom hanging over Goodison Park. But with the club desperately needing money to rebuild the team, he was sold to Newcastle United for £1.4 million during the 1993 close season.

One of the Magpies' all-time great players, he scored 118 goals in 319 League and Cup games in his two spells at St James' Park, and was awarded the MBE in the 1995 Queen's Birthday Honours List. He joined Bolton Wanderers in the summer of 1997 for the promise of first team football but it didn't work out and he was allowed to go on loan, first to Manchester City and then Fulham, helping the Cottagers reach the play-offs. The perfect role model for any youngster to follow, Beardsley later played for Hartlepool United, showing terrific enthusiasm and perfect behaviour on and off the field and it was this coupled with his tremendous ability that kept him at the top for so long. Peter is now a co-commentator on BBC Radio.

> **Honours**
> League Championship
> 1987-88, 1989-90
> FA Cup 1988-89
> Charity Shield 1988, 1989
> 59 England caps

PAUL BRACEWELL

Born	19 July 1962
Birthplace	Heswall
Height	5ft 8ins
Weight	10st 9lbs

Team	Apps	Gls
Stoke City	123 (6)	5
Sunderland	226 (2)	6
Everton	95 (7)	7
Newcastle U	64 (9)	3
Fulham	61 (1)	1

A player who was later destined to win some of the game's major honours, Paul Bracewell began his career with Stoke City where he won a regular place in the Potters' line-up at the age of 18. He was called up to the England Under-21 squad in 1982-83 and became a regular selection for the next two years. However, at the end of his contract he elected to join Sunderland, but after just a year at Roker Park he was signed by Howard Kendall for Everton. Bracewell holds the rare distinction of making his Everton debut at Wembley where he played in the Charity Shield show-piece against Liverpool in August 1984.

In his first season at Goodison, Bracewell was outstanding. He orchestrated Everton's first victorious League Championship for fifteen years and played in the FA Cup Final where the Blues lost in extra-time to Manchester United. He also won the first of three England caps while on a summer tour in North America. He came on as a substitute against West Germany in Mexico in June 1985 and followed this a few days later with a full game against the United States in Los Angeles.

Equally outstanding in 1985-86, Bracewell's season ended in heartache as Everton found the double snatched from their grasp by rivals Liverpool. The Reds took the League Championship with an incredible late surge as the Toffees stumbled - Liverpool also snatched the FA Cup with a second-half 'turnaround' to win 3-1.

Tragically, Bracewell was struck down by a serious injury at the height of his career and did not play first-team

Bracewell holds the rare distinction of making his Everton debut at Wembley

the Wearsiders in the 1992 FA Cup Final, only to once again be on the losing side as Liverpool ran out winners 2-0.

On joining Newcastle United Bracewell made a telling contribution to the Magpies' promotion to the Premier League before returning to Sunderland for his third spell and helping the club return to the top flight as First Division champions.

In October 1997 the veteran midfielder joined Fulham as the club's player-coach and, after helping the Cottagers reach the play-offs in his first season, he was instrumental in the club winning the Second Division Championship in 1998-99. When Kevin Keegan left to manage England, Bracewell took over the reins at Craven Cottage but despite taking Fulham to the fringe of the First Division play-offs, he was sacked. Paul Bracewell is now manager of Halifax Town.

football for two-and-a-half years, only returning in December 1988. Although he played for the remainder of the season, including the 1989 FA Cup Final where he received a losers' medal for the third time, he was a shadow of his former self and in the summer he was allowed to leave and returned to Sunderland. He played for

Honours
League Championship 1984-85
European Cup Winners' Cup 1984-85
3 England caps

KEVIN CAMPBELL

Born	4 February 1970	
Birthplace	Lambeth	
Height	6ft 1ins	
Weight	13st 8lbs	

Team	Apps	Gls
Arsenal	124 (42)	46
L Orient (L)	16	9
Leicester (L)	11	5
Nott'm F	79 (1)	32
Everton	115 (10)	45

A product of the South London Schools in the 1987-88 season, Kevin Campbell smashed all Arsenal goalscoring records, finding the net 59 times for the youth team and was a permanent member of the side that won the FA Youth Cup. This form earned him his League debut on the last day of the season at Goodison Park against Everton.

When the Gunners won the League Championship in 1988-89, Merson and Smith held down the regular striker positions and Campbell was loaned out to Leyton Orient. After further experience on loan to Leicester City, he was given an extended run in the Arsenal side, his form earning him selection for England at Under-21 level.

By now Campbell had become a thoroughbred athlete whose sturdy build was more aligned to

"Last season Campbell finished top scorer and enjoyed the historic honour of being made the first black captain of Everton Football Club."

a middleweight boxer than to a footballer. His great attributes were his physical power, his pace over short distances and his ability to turn defenders when in close control with the ball.

Playing alongside a variety of strikers, he was a member of Arsenal's victorious double Cup winning team of 1992-93, netting four times en route to the final of the European Cup Winners' Cup. Towards the end of his time at Highbury, his form suffered because of a crisis of confidence and in the summer of 1995 he joined Nottingham Forest for a fee of £2.5 million, a figure set by an independent tribunal.

Campbell suffered in his first season at the City Ground with a long-standing back problem but began the 1996-97 season with an opening day hat-trick against Coventry City. He later formed a deadly strike partnership with Pierre Van Hooijdonk which helped Forest win the First Division Championship before leaving for Trabzonspor of Turkey.

Unable to settle, Campbell then exploded on to the Premiership scene in an astonishing loan spell with Everton, which began in transfer deadline week in March 1999. After scoring nine goals in eight games, including a hat-trick in a 6-0 win over West Ham United, Campbell found himself not only the subject of hero worship at Goodison Park but also the club's leading scorer. During the close season the club began moves to make the loan deal permanent and eventually a fee of £3 million was agreed.

In 1999-2000 Campbell led the Blues' forward line with pace, strength and guile. Midway through the season then England manager Kevin Keegan visited Goodison to check on the form of Nick Barmby and Francis Jeffers but he left the ground extolling the virtues of Kevin Campbell after another typical performance by the Everton striker.

Creating a formidable strike partnership with Francis Jeffers, Campbell again ended the campaign as the Blues' top scorer. However Kevin fell victim to a knee injury in March 2000, nevertheless when he hobbled on to the Goodison Park pitch on crutches after the final game of the season, the popular striker received a rousing ovation.

Last season, Campbell was offered neither the service nor the support to produce the form which marked his first full season at Goodison, yet he still finished top scorer and enjoyed the historic honour of being made the first black captain of Everton Football Club.

BOBBY COLLINS

Born	16 February 1931
Birthplace	Glasgow
Height	5ft 4ins
Weight	10st 3lbs

Team	Apps	Gls
Everton	133	42
Leeds U	149	24
Bury	74 (1)	5
Oldham A	6 (1)	0

One of the game's finest inside-forwards, Bobby Collins joined Everton straight from Scottish junior soccer during the reign of Theo Kelly but returned north of the border to sign for Celtic after confessing that he was desperately homesick. In ten years at Parkhead he won a Scottish League Championship medal in 1954, Scottish Cup winners' medals in 1957 and 1958 and appeared for the Scottish League representative side 16 times and remains one of few players to score a hat-trick of penalties (against Aberdeen in September 1953).

During his final season with Celtic, the Scottish international scored heavily and when in September 1958 he joined Everton for £23,000, he was initially employed as a front man. In fact, Collins made his debut for the Blues only hours after putting pen to paper, scoring a goal in a 3-1 win over Manchester City at Maine Road. Quickly

"Collins' supreme talent was to make the Blues play, dictating the pattern of games with his crisp, incisive passes."

however, he expressed his need for more constant involvement and adopted a much deeper lying role. Nicknamed 'the Little General' he became captain under the Blues' newly appointed team boss Johnny Carey and for two seasons was arguably the major factor in the club retaining their top flight status. As well as setting up untold opportunities for his fellow forwards, he top-scored with 14 goals in 1959-60 and went three better the following season when his total included hat-tricks in home games against Newcastle United (5-0) and Cardiff City (5-1).

Collins' supreme talent was to make the Blues play, dictating the pattern of games with his crisp, incisive passes. He loved the ball, using it to pick out his team-mates in dangerous positions with astonishing accuracy. He was quick too, with impeccable control and it was a great pity when this complete footballer was allowed to leave Goodison Park in

March 1962, joining Leeds United for £25,000.

Bobby Collins was the platform on which Don Revie launched his great sixties side. He went on to turn a mediocre club from the depths of Division Two into one of the most respected in Europe. He captained Leeds to the Second Division title in 1963-64 and the following season was voted Footballer of the Year as United came close to the League and Cup double. He was also recalled to the Scottish side after an absence of six years. Collins broke a thigh bone in United's first European tie in Turin but recovered well.

He left Elland Road on a free transfer to join Bury and then embarked on a journey which took in Morton and Australian clubs Ringwood and Hakoah. He had a spell with Shamrock Rovers, followed by Oldham Athletic, where he was the Boundary Park club's player-coach before stepping up to assistant-manager. He was in his 43rd year when he made his final League appearance for the Latics.

Collins later held a number of coaching and management posts before leaving the game to spend eight years working in the wholesale fashion business. Now retired after two years working at Leeds University as a driver, he still plays in the occasional charity match.

**Honours:
31 Scotland caps**

TONY COTTEE

Born	11 July 1965	
Birthplace	West Ham	
Height	5ft 9ins	
Weight	12st 6 lbs	

Team	Apps	Gls
West Ham	266 (13)	115
Everton	161 (23)	72
Leicester City	66 (17)	27
Birmingham C	4 (1)	1
Norwich City	5 (2)	1
Barnet	16 (9)	9
Millwall	0 (2)	0

After following the Hammers as a young boy, Tony Cottee went to Upton Park as an apprentice, having been spotted by West Ham scout Ronnie Gale while playing for Chase Cross United. He made a sensational first team debut, scoring after 26 minutes in the match against Tottenham Hotspur on New Year's Day 1983, aged 17.

In 1985-86, Cottee was capped for the England Under-21 team, won the PFA and Fiat Uno Young Player of the Year awards and was voted Hammer of the Year. After winning full international honours against Sweden, he returned to Upton Park and three days later netted his first hat-trick for the club against Queen's Park Rangers, quickly following it with another against Coventry City.

In the summer of 1988, Colin Harvey's prolonged search for a forward capable of combining skill and a natural predatory instinct ended when he beat off the challenge of Arsenal to sign Cottee for a then British transfer record of £2.3 million. Cottee quickly settled into a talented if somewhat inconsistent Everton side and marked his debut with a magnificent hat-trick in a 4-0 home win over Newcastle United on the opening day of the 1988-89 season - his first goal coming after just 34 seconds! Although he ended his first season on Merseyside as the Blues leading scorer and helped the club reach the FA Cup Final. Cottee's team-mates were often guilty of not playing to his particular strengths. In fact, he was the club's leading scorer in five of the six seasons he spent at Goodison and though there were times when he had outstanding spells while playing alongside the likes of Sharp and Newell, Beardsley and Rideout, he never really found his ideal foil.

"Cottee was the club's leading scorer in five of the six seasons he spent at Goodison"

City. The most prolific West Ham striker since Geoff Hurst, he was surprisingly allowed to join Selengor of Malaysia, later returning to play for Leicester City.

In his first season with the Foxes, Cottee was finally able to fulfil one ambition by playing in a European competition. In 1998-99 he scored all three goals in the club's two-legged Worthington Cup semi-final victory over Sunderland but Leicester were beaten by Spurs in the final. He finally achieved his ambition of collecting a winners' medal at Wembley the following season as the Foxes beat Tranmere Rovers to lift the League Cup.

On leaving Filbert Street, Cottee had a brief spell with Norwich City before becoming player-manager of Barnet. But despite scoring after only minutes of his debut against Blackpool in a 7-0 win, he later lost his job as the club slid towards the Conference. He completed his trip around the divisions by joining Second Division promotion candidates Millwall but was released in the summer of 2001.

During his stay at Goodison Park, Cottee constantly found himself at odds with the manager and on one occasion was fined £5,000 after refusing to play in a reserve team fixture against Coventry City at Highfield Road.

The Blues should have made much more of their expensive investment, but in September 1994, Cottee left Goodison Park to rejoin West Ham United. Though he was sent-off at Liverpool in the first match of his second spell, he ended the season as the club's top scorer, netting another hat-trick against Manchester

Honours
7 England Caps

MARTIN DOBSON

Born	14 March 1951	
Birthplace	Glasgow	
Height	5ft 8ins	
Weight	11st 13 lbs	

Team	Apps	Gls
Burnley	406 (4)	63
Everton	190	29
Bury	60 (1)	4

Honours
5 England Caps

One of the game's most elegant and stylish footballers, Martin Dobson was very nearly lost to the professional game when Bolton Wanderers gave him a free transfer in 1967. It was crushing blow to the young man and he was on the point of giving up the game when his father persuaded Burnley manager Harry Potts to give him a trial.

Dobson impressed sufficiently to be offered a contract and initially disputed the striking roles with Willie Irvine and Andy Lochhead. Later a loss of form for Colin Waldron prompted Potts to try him at centre-half. Such was the impression he made that he won England Under-23 honours in that position. Eventually he moved into midfield and was appointed club captain, skippering the Clarets to the Second Division Championship in 1972-73. The following season he led Burnley to sixth place in the top flight and to an FA Cup semi-final after which he arrived on the full international stage in what was Alf Ramsey's last match as England manager.

One of the Clarets' prized assets, Dobson left Turf Moor for Everton in August 1979, the Blues smashing the British transfer record by paying £300,000 for the midfielder's services. He made his debut for the Blues in a 2-1 home win over Arsenal and though he was only on the losing side once in his first spell of 16 games, it took him a considerable length of time to settle into his new role.

Dobson graced the Everton midfield for five campaigns, prompting intelligently and contributing some fiercely struck goals, none more so than the piledriver that climaxed a 40-yard run in the Merseyside derby at Anfield in October 1976.

He figured in two UEFA Cup campaigns and in 1977 played in the FA Cup semi-final defeat by Liverpool and the three-game marathon in the League Cup Final which ended in defeat to Aston Villa at Old Trafford. In the 1978-79 League Cup campaign he scored a hat-trick when Everton achieved their best scoreline in the competition, 8-0 against

Wimbledon in a second round tie - Bob Latchford hitting the other five.

Highly skilful and with the ability to drift forward to create openings and goals out of next-to-nothing, Dobson won just one more full cap as an Everton player.

It was something of a surprise when, at the age of 31, Dobson returned to Turf Moor in the summer of 1979 for £100,000. During his second spell with the Clarets, he captained the side to the Third Division championship in 1981-82. However, following the appointment of John Bond, Dobson moved to Bury, later becoming player-manager. He led the Shakers to promotion from Division Four but after a disagreement with the board he left to take charge of Bristol Rovers.

Now over three decades after leaving Bolton, Dobson is back with the Wanderers as the club's Youth Development Officer.

Derby Facts

Here are some facts about Everton's League games against Liverpool since the two first met in 1894.

* The longest unbeaten run in matches home and away is 14, held by Everton.

* The longest unbeaten run in home matches is held by Liverpool when Everton failed to beat them in the League for 14 games between the 1970/71 season and 1984-85.

* The longest unbeaten run away from home is held by Everton with an astonishing 15 match run at Anfield between 1899 and 1920 which included 10 victories.

* The longest unbroken winning run at home belongs to Liverpool with 5 between 1932-33 and 1936-37.

* The longest unbroken winning run away from home belongs to Everton who scored 7 consecutive victories at Anfield between 1908-09 and 1914-1915.

* The record victory in a league match is 6-0 recorded by Liverpool at Goodison Park in the 1935-36 season.

TOMMY EGLINGTON

Born	15 January 1923	
Birthplace	Dublin	
Height	5ft 11ins	
Weight	11st 6 lbs	

Team	Apps	Gls
Everton	394	76
Tranmere R	172	36

One of Everton's greatest-ever servants, Tommy Eglington also stands out as one of the early giants of Irish football. Like many of his contemporaries, he excelled at hurling and Gaelic football during his schooldays but it was as one of the finest match-winning left-wingers in the game of football that he came to be remembered.

Eglington joined Everton in the summer of 1946 in a double transfer deal involving the Blues' other immediate post-war great, Peter Farrell. The double deal, which cost Everton £10,000, has often been described as the best piece of business in the club's history.

Elegant and unruffled, with an explosive burst of pace and a thundering shot, Eglington had been with Shamrock Rovers for just one full season, 1945-46, ending the campaign as the Hoops' top-scorer with 11 goals before he departed for Goodison Park.

Eglington made his League debut for the Blues in a 3-2 home win over Arsenal in September 1946, going on to claim a regular place in the Everton side almost immediately. He kept his place for the next eleven seasons all but three of which were spent in the top flight.

Following the Blues' relegation in the 1950-51 season they were promoted back to Division One at the end of 1953-54, having finished as runners-up to Leicester City on goal difference.

During this spell at the lower level, Eglington guaranteed himself a place in the pages of Everton's history when, on 27 September 1952, he almost single-handedly demolished Doncaster Rovers at Goodison Park by scoring five Toffees goals in a 7-1 win. He ended

"on 27 September 1952, he almost single-handedly demolished Doncaster Rovers at Goodison Park scoring five goals in a 7-1 win"

that season as the club's leading scorer in the Football League with 14 goals in 39 games.

One of only a handful of players who have appeared for both Northern Ireland and the Republic, he was a member of the Irish side which recorded an historic 2-0 victory over an England side - appropriately enough at Goodison Park - in 1949 when they became the first overseas side to defeat England on English soil.

Eglington made six appearances for Northern Ireland between 1946 and 1948 and he was the Republic's regular outside-right for a decade in the immediate post-war years. During that time he won 24 caps, scored two goals and was national team captain twice.

A player with intricate close control and stunning shooting power, Eglington left Everton for Tranmere Rovers in the summer of 1957. For three seasons he gave the Birkenhead club the same wholehearted service that he had given the Blues, scoring 36 goals in 172 outings in Division Three (North). When he finally hung up his boots, Eglington returned to his native Dublin where he ran a butcher's shop.

Honours
24 Republic of Ireland
& 6 Northern Ireland Caps

PETER FARRELL

Born	16 August 1923	
Birthplace	Dublin	
Height	5ft 9ins	
Weight	10st 12 lbs	

Team	Apps	Gls
Everton	422	13
Tranmere R	114	1

P eter Farrell's career coincided with that of Tommy Eglington, for after playing with Shamrock Rovers as a schoolboy, the two of them joined Everton in a combined deal which cost the Blues £10,000 spread over two years. Like his close friend Eglington, Farrell enjoyed eleven seasons with Everton, during which time he became something of a living legend on Merseyside, being one of the few footballers to have a street named after him - Farrell Close.

His debut for Everton was postponed until late November 1946 because of an injury he sustained while playing tennis. After that, he was a virtual ever-present in the Everton side, though on 22 September 1956, for the match against Sunderland which the Blues won 2-1, the club decided to give

> **"In eleven seasons with Everton, Farrell became something of a living legend on Merseyside, being one of the few footballers to have a street named after him - Farrell Close."**

Farrell a well-earned rest, affording one reporter the opportunity to pa tribute to 'one of the most loyal servant the Goodison Park club has ever see in its long history....Personally I thin his inspiration and experience will be missed....as captain there have bee few as good and none bette always giving his last ounce to the cause.'

On the internationa front, Farrel appeared at left half for Northern Ireland in seve international between Septembe 1946 and March 1949 while he was a regular i the Republic of Ireland side from 1946 to 1957, making a total o 28 appearances. He scored one o the goals in the Republic's epic 2-0 defeat of England at Goodison Park in September 1949, making them the first overseas team to beat England

In October 1957, less than six months after Eglington left Everton for Tranmere Rovers, Peter Farrell embarked on the same short journey across the River Mersey to link up yet again with his close friend and colleague. He was immediately appointed captain at Prenton Park and although his three seasons on the Wirral were not the happiest of his career, he continued to play as enthusiastically as ever, more than justifying Tranmere's £2,500 investment in a player heading towards the end of his career.

Farrell left Tranmere at the end of 1960 to join Welsh non-League side Hdyhist Town as player-manager, later returning to Ireland to continue in management before working in broadcasting with RTE in Dublin.

on English soil. Farrell also achieved the unusual honour of captaining his country in his first international, an honour bestowed on him in a further 11 internationals.

Farrell was Everton captain when the Blues dropped down to Division Two in 1950-51 for only the second time in their history. However, their fall from grace was short-lived for three seasons later they found their way back into the top flight.

An inspiration to all around him and very popular on the field, Farrell was also something of a hero off it, mixing freely with the club's supporters in a down-to-earth manner.

DUNCAN FERGUSON

Born	27 December 1971
Birthplace	Stirling
Height	6ft 4ins
Weight	14st 6 lbs

Team	Apps	Gls
Everton	136 (21)	49
Newcastle U	24 (6)	8

Big Dunc soon showed that he was one of the hottest young talents in Britain when he began his career with Dundee United. He was a rarity in the domestic game, a highly skilled big forward, good on the ground and in the air. Under the oppressive reign of Jim McLean, he found it hard to feel comfortable and had various brushes with the Tannadice taskmaster, including walk-outs and public slanging matches.

In the summer of 1993, Ferguson became the most expensive footballer in Britain as Rangers shelled out £3.75 million for his services. After an injury-blighted debut season, his first goal against Raith Rovers was forgotten about as he earned a police charge and a record 12 game ban from the SFA for a headbutting offence on John McStay. He was subsequently sentenced to three months in jail.

When the then Rangers manager Walter Smith let him go on loan to Everton for three months, his form,

though solid enough, suggested that the Blues would be happy to stick to that agreement too. It was only when Joe Royle took charge that the big man took off and two goals in his opening four games, including a derby strike against Liverpool, made their minds up.

Everton paid £4.3 million for Ferguson and over the next few months he proved a key element in the Blues' rise from the foot of the table. He also won an FA Cup winners' medal when, despite labouring with a groin problem, he came on as a second-half substitute against Manchester United.

Sadly the 1995-96 season was a personal nightmare for the Everton target man as continual niggling injuries dogged him from the outset of the campaign. The following season he reserved his best performances for the big matches, scoring spectacular goals at Old Trafford and in the Goodison derby match. He also returned to international duty for Scotland, winning caps against Austria and Estonia in World Cup qualifying matches.

Blues' manager Howard Kendall seemed to have pulled a master-stroke of psychology midway through the 1997-98 season when he named

Ferguson as captain. In his first match as skipper, he scored a hat-trick of headers against Bolton and netted another goal against arch rivals Liverpool at Anfield. During the closing weeks of the campaign, he played on with a knee injury before informing the Scottish FA he no longer wished to be considered for selection for the international side.

In November 1998, Ferguson, who had become the idol of the Goodison crowd, joined Newcastle United for £7 million. The unrest following his signing for the Magpies led to the resignation of Everton chairman Peter Johnson.

The 'Toon Army' were looking forward to his partnership with Alan Shearer but the England striker was injured at the time of Big Dunc's arrival and when he returned it was Ferguson's turn to suffer with a wide range of injuries. In fact, much of Ferguson's time on Tyneside was injury-ridden before he returned to Goodison Park for a second spell.

The Everton hit man wasn't as prolific as he would have liked because he again suffered from a cruel spate of injuries. Yet his goals-to-games return is one that only a few other top-flight strikers can better. All Evertonians will be hoping that the new season is an injury-free one for the popular Scotsman.

Honours
FA Cup 1994-5
7 Scotland caps

WALLY FIELDING

Born	26 November 1919
Birthplace	Edmonton
Height	5ft 9ins
Weight	11st 11 lbs

Team	Apps	Gls
Everton	380	49
Southport	20	1

D ubbed 'Merseyside's answer to Len Shackleton', Wally Fielding was at the centre of a row when he signed professional forms at Goodison Park in 1945. Before he joined the army, Wally Fielding was on Charlton Athletic's books as an amateur. He went to the Middle East where his form as a scheming inside-forward was good enough to get him into army representative sides. When he left the army, Charlton believed that they held the right to his continued services. But despite the attentions of numerous other leading clubs of the day, he opted to join Everton and started a furious debate which was to last for many months.

After making his Blues' debut in a 2-0 home defeat at the hands of Brentford on the opening day of the 1946-47 season, Fielding made the No 10

"Fielding was a huge influence on Everton youngsters, who loved to copy his mannerism of clutching his rolled-down shirt sleeves as he ran."

shirt his own over the next twelve years. Everton had acquired not only a strategist who became the starting point of numerous attacks but also a marksman who carried an accurate and powerful shot. He came close to netting a hat-trick in the game against Aston Villa in September 1947 - after scoring the first two goals in Everton's 3-0 win, the shot that would have given him the feat cannoned off a Villa defender and went down as an own goal.

One of Fielding's trademarks was his perfectly weighted passes inside the full-back to Tommy Eglington. He was also more than capable of looking after himself in the face of the most ferocious tackle. If he did have a fault, it was his lack of pace but few would disagree that he was most unlucky never to win full international honours for England.

fact he did make one appearance in the white shirt of England, playing in the Bolton Wanderers Disaster Fund match against Scotland at Manchester in 1946 - a game that did not count as an official full cap.

Invariably known as 'Nobby', Wally Fielding was one of the game's chirpiest characters and was adored by the Everton faithful. There was no doubt that he was a huge influence on the Goodison club's youngsters, who loved to copy his mannerism of clutching his rolled-down shirt sleeves as he ran.

When the Londoner left Goodison Park in the summer of 1959, he was approaching forty years of age, yet he was still bubbling with enthusiasm. He joined Southport as the Haig Avenue club's player-manager. Unfortunately he was not a great success as the Sandgrounders had to seek re-election in 1959-60. In fact, they were in financial difficulties and were lucky not to be voted out of the League, a fate that befell Gateshead instead.

On leaving Southport, Fielding moved south to become trainer-coach at Luton Town before being appointed Watford's youth coach. He later ended his involvement with the game after a spell as Luton's chief scout.

JIMMY GABRIEL

Born	16 October 1940
Birthplace	Dundee
Height	5ft 10ins
Weight	11st 12 lbs

Team	Apps	Gls
Everton	255 (1)	33
Southampton	190 (1)	25
Bournemouth	53	4
Swindon T (L)	6	0
Brentford	9	0

A powerhouse of a right-half, Jimmy Gabriel became one of the most expensive teenagers in British football when he arrived at Goodison Park from Dundee for £30,000 in March 1960. He made his Everton debut against West Ham United only 72 hours after putting pen to paper, coming south of the border just a year after his compatriot Dave Mackay, who had been an inspiration to Spurs.

Understandably the young Gabriel needed time to settle and in only his third senior outing he was given a fearful run-around by West Bromwich Albion's England international Derek Kevan who scored five times as Everton were beaten 6-2 at the Hawthorns. However, Gabriel reacted positively, volunteering for extra training to hone his fitness, as he began to acclimatise to the more rigorous demands of the English game.

Gabriel went on to build a fine career for himself. His strong forceful style, particularly effective in defence, made him the near-perfect foil for the more adventurous wanderings of Brian Harris on the opposite flank. However, there were times when he contributed several stirring performances as an emergency centre-forward, scoring from this position in the 3-1 victory over Liverpool in February 1964.

When Brian Harris lost his place to Tony Kay midway through the 1962-63 season, Gabriel continued to complement his midfield partner helping the Blues win the League Championship. He was also a leading light in the club's 1966 FA Cup Final victory over Sheffield Wednesday. Few will forget the Scottish international's gap-toothed grin and sweat-soaked shirt at the end of the Blues' 3-2 win.

Despite such success, Gabriel was not destined to see out his prime with the Goodison club. The date 18 March 1967 marked the beginning of the end of his Everton career. On that day he was sent to Blackpool with

the reserves while newcomer Howard Kendall made his League debut against Southampton.

Only 26 years old, Gabriel was sold to Southampton the following summer where he contributed five years' yeoman service. He was just the sort of player Saints needed at that time and when he left to play for Bournemouth in July 1972 he was sorely missed. After just over a year with the Dean Court club, he moved to North America where he played for Seattle Sounders.

In the summer of 1990 Gabriel returned to Goodison Park to help Blues' manager Colin Harvey look after the first team, later taking over as caretaker boss at either end of Howard Kendall's second reign. Despite all the managerial changes at Everton, Jimmy Gabriel remained part of the coaching set-up and exerted a particularly valuable influence on the Blues' youngsters until he left Goodison in the summer of 1997 and headed for the United States. However, it is as an accomplished top-flight performer when the Blues had their backs to the wall that Everton fans will forever remember Jimmy Gabriel.

> **Honours**
> **League Championship 1962-63**
> **FA Cup 1965-66**
> **2 Scotland caps**

ANDY GRAY

Born	30 November 1955	
Birthplace	Glasgow	
Height	5ft 11ins	
Weight	11st 13 lbs	

Team	Apps	Gls
Aston Villa	165 (3)	59
Wolves	130 (3)	38
Everton	44 (5)	14
Notts Co (L)	3 (1)	0
West Brom	32 (3)	10

One of the bravest strikers of his generation, Andy Gray began his career with Dundee United, scoring 44 goals in 76 games for the Tannadice club before moving to Aston Villa for £110,000 in September 1975. In 1976-77 when Villa finished fourth in Division One and beat Everton in the League Cup Final, Gray was the club's leading scorer with 29 goals. He became the first man in the history of the game to receive both the Player of the Year and the Young Player of the Year awards in the same season from the Professional Footballers' Association.

After four years at Villa Park, he moved to Wolverhampton Wanderers for a British record fee of £1.5 million and made his debut at Goodison, scoring in Wanderers' 3-2 victory. But his career seemed to be going nowhere at Molineux and Everton manager Howard Kendall was able to secure his services for just £250,000 in November 1983.

Gray was prone to injury and many considered him too old when he arrived at Goodison Park. It took some weeks to make his presence felt but he went on to display a new zest for the game, proving to be an important and exciting capture. A very special relationship was forged between Andy Gray and the Everton fans, as he became one of the inspirational figures behind the Blues' great eighties revival.

During that 1983-84 season, Gray was cup-tied and unavailable for action in the Milk Cup but was very much involved in the FA Cup. In the sixth round at Meadow Lane, he scored a remarkable winner to defeat Notts County. Launching himself along the

> "Gray certainly left his mark on Everton Football Club, following in the footsteps of Dean, Lawton, Royle and Latchford."

he scored the first goal in a 3-1 defeat of the Austrian side, Gray was dramatically recalled into the Scotland side, eventually ending with 20 full caps to his name.

In July 1985 he was allowed to return to Aston Villa as the Blues signed Gary Lineker. The Goodison faithful sent petitions to manager Kendall to record their great disappointment at his departure. He had certainly left his mark on Everton Football Club, following in the footsteps of Dean, Lawton, Royle and Latchford. His stay at Goodison was comparatively short yet he scored some crucial goals and inspired all those around him.

After a loan spell at Notts County, Gray signed for West Bromwich Albion but retired shortly after his arrival at the Hawthorns. In the summer of 1991 he returned to Villa Park for a third time as assistant-manager to Ron Atkinson. He resigned in 1992 to pursue a career in television with Sky Sports.

slippery ground, he made contact with the ball only inches from the surface to send a superb diving header inside Mick Lennards's right-hand post. In the final against Watford, he scored one of the goals in Everton's 2-0 triumph. Many people thought he fouled the Vicarage Road club's goalkeeper Steve Sherwood when he jumped for the ball in front of the posts but as the video shows, Gray never touched him.

After playing his part in the League Championship success of 1984-85 and the European Cup Winners' Cup victory over Rapid Vienna in Rotterdam where

Honours
League Championship 1984-85
FA Cup 1983-84
European Cup Winners' Cup 1984-85
20 Scotland caps

BRIAN HARRIS

Born	16 May 1935	
Birthplace	Bebington	
Height	5ft 9ins	
Weight	11st 10 lbs	

Team	Apps	Gls
Everton	310	23
Cardiff City	147 [2]	0
Newport Co.	85	0

One of the game's most underrated footballers, Brian Harris was a winger when he arrived at Goodison Park from non-League Port Sunlight in January 1954. Making his debut in a 1-0 win at Burnley during the early part of the 1955-56 season, Harris contributed a number of lively performances and a smattering of goals. However, he only began to develop his full potential after he had been converted to the wing-half position in 1958. Though he was right-footed, Harris was destined to make the majority of his Everton appearances on the left because of the need to accommodate the talented Jimmy Gabriel.

As a wing-half Harris's skill and vision were supplemented by a ferocious tackle, good aerial ability and a powerful shot. Though the majority of his duties were defensive, he specialised in early balls that frequently caught opposing defenders unawares. In this deep-lying role, he played an important part in Everton's transformation from a club struggling at the foot of the First Division to one of the major powers in British football.

Even when the Blues could afford to compete at the top of the transfer market, Harris still held down a first-team place until he was axed following the signing of Tony Kay from Sheffield Wednesday for £55,000 in December 1962. That season the Blues went on to win the League Championship and while many other players might have responded with a transfer request, Harris elected to stay and fight for his place.

Though the circumstances in which he regained his first-team spot - the bribes

> *"In his deep-lying role, he played an important part in Everton's transformation from a club struggling at the foot of the First Division to one of the major powers in British football.*

scandal which resulted in Kay's imprisonment - were somewhat bizarre, the fact remains that Everton boss Harry Catterick rated the wing-half very highly to give him three more seasons of top flight football.

Harris's greatest personal triumph came at Wembley in 1966 when, just two days short of his 31st birthday, he gave a commanding display to help the Blues overturn a two-goal Sheffield Wednesday lead on the way to lifting the FA Cup.

In the eleven years Harris was at Goodison, he played in every position except goalkeeper for the first team and in so doing still maintained a degree of consistency that few so-called 'stars' came close to emulating.

In the October following the Cup Final victory, Harris left Everton to join Cardiff City. No stranger to European soccer, having played in Everton's early European Cup and Fairs Cup games, he played in all nine of Cardiff's 1967-68 European Cup Winners' Cup games when they just missed out on reaching the final. He left Cardiff in the summer of 1971 to become player-manager of Newport County. After almost leading them to promotion in his first season at Somerton

Park, he resigned after a disagreement with the board over finances.

Harris later returned to Ninian Park as assistant-manager to Richie Morgan, a post he held for two years. He now runs his own promotions business in South Wales.

Honours
League Championship 1962-63
FA Cup 1965-66

JIMMY HARRIS

Born	18 August 1933	
Birthplace	Birkenhead	
Height	5ft 11ins	
Weight	11st 12 lbs	

Team	Apps	Gls
Everton	191	65
Birmingham C	93	37
Oldham Ath.	28 (1)	9

A member of the successful Birkenhead Schools' side, Jimmy Harris first came to the Blues' notice on the say-so of his aunt, who reckoned that his 60 goals in a season must qualify her prolific nephew for a trial! He progressed rapidly and in August 1955 he was called up unexpectedly to replace the injured Dave Hickson for the game against Burnley. It was Harris who caused panic in the Clarets' defence, allowing Tommy Jones to score the game's only goal.

"his pace, control and lethal finishing power set the Goodison terraces alight."

Harris kept his place in the side, his pace, control and lethal finishing power setting the Goodison terraces alight. Midway through his first season in the side, he was rewarded with an England Under-23 cap when he played against Scotland at Hillsborough. He ended the campaign as the club's leading scorer with 21 League and Cup goals.

Sadly in 1956-57 injuries and a loss of form limited his appearances and some critics thought the lightly-built striker lacked the necessary physical presence. Remarkably the return of Dave Hickson from his transfer travels revived his flagging fortunes. He moved out to the right-wing position, occasionally turning out at inside-right, his goal touch returning.

When Everton met Spurs at White Hart Lane in October 1958, Harris notched a splendid hat-trick. Understandably he wasn't too impressed with the efforts of his team-mates as the Blues went down 10-4!

Though the Blues were struggling in the lower reaches of the First Division, Harris's performances were impressive and he continued to score his fair share of goals. His displays led to him being picked for the Football League, but shortly afterwards Hickson left Goodison for rivals Liverpool and Harris resumed his central position.

Everton had made a successful start to the 1960-61 season, losing just two of their opening eighteen games but Harris, who was playing up front alongside Roy Vernon, had only scored four goals. So when Everton manager Harry Catterick signed Alex Young, Harris knew that his first team days at Goodison were numbered. A month later he joined Birmingham City, choosing the St Andrews club instead of West Bromwich Albion because he knew City's trainer Tommy Jones from his days with Birkenhead Schools.

Harris scored on his City debut in a 5-0 win over Boldklub of Copenhagen in the Fairs Cup, while his first League game was against the Blues at St Andrews, an entertaining game which Everton won 4-2. Harris ended his first season at the club as the leading scorer with 13 goals. He repeated the feat in 1961-62 with 20 goals while his only honour with City was a League Cup winners' tankard in 1963 as Aston Villa were beaten in the two-legged final.

In July 1964 Harris signed for Oldham Athletic, moving to Tranmere Rovers two years later. Unable to break into the club's League side, he left the game to become steward at nearby Prenton Golf Club.

COLIN HARVEY

Born	16 November 1944
Birthplace	Liverpool
Height	5ft 7ins
Weight	11st 0 lbs

Team	Apps	Gls
Everton	317 (3)	18
Sheffield Wed.	45	2

As a youngster Colin Harvey had a trial with Liverpool and was told to come back the following week, but in the meantime he was invited for a trial at Goodison. Offered professional terms, he jumped at the chance, thoroughly enjoying the discipline and training that were part of a football apprentice's life.

With Jimmy Gabriel injured, Everton manager Harry Catterick was forced to give a debut to the homegrown 18-year-old Harvey in the second leg of the European Cup first round tie against Inter Milan in the San Siro Stadium. The first leg at Goodison had been goalless and though Harvey played with a maturity and experience, Everton lost the return to the only goal of the game.

After that baptism of fire, Harvey managed just two First Division games that season but established himself in the side in 1964-65 after playing in a tough encounter with Manchester United in mid-September. Two days later he played in his first Merseyside derby, Everton beating their arch rivals 4-0 with Harvey getting on the scoresheet. He played in 32 games that season as the Blues ended the campaign in fourth place. In 1966 Everton played League champions Manchester United in the FA Cup semi-final at Burnden Park. The Blues soaked up the United pressure and then counter-attacked with Colin Harvey shooting them into the final where they beat Sheffield Wednesday 3-2.

Colin Harvey's finest quality was his vision and his ability to spray long accurate passes to his forwards, while at the same time he would effectively block any impending attacks by the opposition through his brilliant positional play. Yet he won only one England cap and that was in 1971 when Malta were beaten 1-0.

Harvey was the stabilising influence in the magnificent midfield trio that was instrumental in Everton winning the 1969-70 League Championship. Though slightly built, he won the ball in tackles with the great timing of his challenges. He gave everything in a match; he didn't know how to play it any other way - he was the sort of player that all managers would love to have in their team.

In October 1974 Harvey was allowed to leave Goodison and joined Sheffield Wednesday for £70,000. Sadly, a niggling hip injury caught up with him late in his career and two years after arriving at Hillsborough he was forced to retire. He resumed his links with Everton through the coaching ranks where, despite having a hip replacement, he took a full active role in the training programme.

There is no doubt that he can take much of the credit for Everton's success in the mid-1980s but he was not cut out to be a manager. When he succeeded Howard Kendall in the summer of 1987 he seemed almost reluctant to do so,

knowing deep down that it was not the right role for him. He was dismissed at the end of October 1990 but six days later he returned to Goodison as assistant manager following the re-appointment of Howard Kendall. Harvey later left Goodison to become assistant manager to Graeme Sharp at Oldham Athletic before both former Blues resigned their posts in February 1997.

Honours
League Championship 1969-70
FA Cup 1965-66
1 England Cap

ADRIAN HEATH

Born	11 January 1961
Birthplace	Stoke
Height	5ft 6ins
Weight	10st 1 lbs

Team	Apps	Gls
Stoke City	99 (2)	18
Everton	206 (20)	71
Aston Villa	8 (1)	0
Man City	58 (17)	4
Burnley	110 (10)	29
Sheffield Utd	8 (4)	0

As an apprentice with his home-town club Stoke City, Adrian Heath was one of a number of local players groomed at the Victoria Ground in the late 1970s. Though he appeared briefly during the Potters' Second Division promotion-winning season of 1978-79, it was the following season before he established himself in the club's midfield, replacing Howard Kendall, who had departed for Blackburn Rovers.

Heath was not a prolific goalscorer during his time at Stoke but his industrious play brought him his first taste of international honours when in April 1981 he lined up in England's Under 21 side to play Romania, scoring twice in a 3-0 win. The following January in the week of his 21st birthday, he was transferred to Everton for a Goodison Park record fee of £700,000.

'Inchy' became an automatic choice in the Everton side and his goalscoring output increased considerably over his days at Stoke. Playing alongside Graeme Sharp, he was the Blues' top scorer in 1983-84 with 18 goals in the League and Cup as the club swept all before them in the FA Cup, collecting the trophy for he first time in eighteen years as Watford were overcome in the Wembley final. One of his most important strikes was the late League Cup equaliser at Oxford - which appeared to revitalise the Blues' flagging fortunes - and though Everton almost made it a Wembley double, they eventually fell to Liverpool in the League Cup Final at Maine Road after a replay.

In 1984-85 the Blues came within ninety minutes of an unprecedented treble, although because of a wrenched knee Heath played only a supporting role in the European Cup Winners' Cup triumph against Rapid Vienna in Rotterdam. He missed the entire FA Cup run to the final, which Manchester United won by the only goal and was then resigned to watching his team-

mates clinch the League Championship.

Everton finished as runners-up to Liverpool in both the League and FA Cup in 1986 but in 1987 won the League Championship again with Heath playing a key role. The following season was a disappointment for both Heath and Everton and in November 1988 he decided to try his luck in Spain, signing for Espanol of Barcelona. However, after less than a year he returned for a short spell with Aston Villa before linking up with Howard Kendall again in February 1990, this time at Manchester City.

In March 1992 he returned to Stoke City but in August that year he joined Burnley. Playing as an out-and-out striker, Heath was soon among the goals and his 20 in his first season at Turf Moor was easily the best of his League career.

He was a key figure in the Clarets' run to promotion via the play-offs in 1994 but after injury restricted his appearances, he accepted the challenge of the position of assistant-manager at Sheffield United where the new manager was none other than Howard Kendall.

Heath later returned to Burnley as manager but in the summer of 1997 he returned to Goodison as first-team coach.

Honours
League Championship 1984-85
FA Cup 1983-84

DAVE HICKSON

Born	30 October 1929	
Birthplace	Salford	
Height	6ft 0 ins	
Weight	12st 6 lbs	

Team	Apps	Gls
Everton	225	95
Aston Villa	12	1
Huddersfield T	54	28
Liverpool	60	37
Bury	8	0
Tranmere R	45	21

The only player to have represented all three Merseyside clubs at first team level, Dave Hickson played his early football for non-League Ellesmere Port. However, after crossing the Mersey to join the Goodison cause in the summer of 1948, he found his progress interrupted by National Service. It was while playing for Cheshire Army Cadets that he was coached by the legendary Dixie Dean. After two years in khaki, Hickson returned to an Everton team that had just been relegated to the Second Division.

Hickson made his League debut for the Blues against Leeds United in September 1951, replacing the injured Harry Catterick. That season he went on to knock in 14 goals, his scoring prowess being largely instrumental in Everton's promotion back to the top flight three seasons later.

However, it was in 1952-53 that Hickson enjoyed the most memorable game of his Everton career. The Blues, who were then still a Second Division club, were drawn at home to Manchester United in the fifth round of the FA Cup. United took the lead after 27 minutes but Tommy Eglington equalised shortly afterwards. Just before half-time, Hickson was taken off the pitch with such a badly cut eye that no one expected him to appear for the second half - but appear he did. Twice the referee suggested he should go

in the closing stages.

In September 1955, Hickson was sold to Aston Villa but after just two months he moved to Huddersfield Town where he came under the managership of Bill Shankly. In August 1957 he rejoined Everton for a bargain £7,500 and was soon back to his brave goalscoring ways.

However in November 1959 Hickson joined Liverpool in one of the most sensational transfer tales in footballing history. Many Evertonians said they would never watch the Blues again; Liverpool supporters vowed not to watch the Reds while Hickson was playing for the team. But Hickson eventually became a hero after scoring both goals in a 2-1 win over Aston Villa, helping Liverpool finish third in Division Two with his prolific goalscoring contribution. He helped the Reds win promotion the following season but found himself surplus to requirements after the arrival of Ian St John.

Hickson then joined Bury before finishing his League career at Tranmere Rovers. He had a brief flirtation as player-manager with Ballymena but a troublesome injury caused him to call it a day.

off but his request was waved aside. Hickson's bravery was rewarded when after 63 minutes he scored the winning goal. Another ball came over and he got in another header that hit the post. The wound opened up again and there was blood everywhere but that did not matter as the Blues were through to the sixth round. He later notched the only goal of the quarter-final against Aston Villa to set up a semi-final meeting with Bolton Wanderers. Though the Blues were 4-0 down at half-time, they staged a remarkable comeback to lose 4-3 with Bolton hanging on grimly

ANDY HINCHCLIFFE

Born	5 February 1969
Birthplace	Manchester
Height	5ft 10 ins
Weight	13 st 7 lbs

Team	Apps	Gls
Man City	107 (5)	8
Everton	170 (12)	7
Sheff Wed	86	7

Andy Hinchcliffe began his Football League career with Manchester City, making his debut against Plymouth Argyle in August 1987. After missing just two games that season, he played a prominent part in the club's promotion to the First Division in 1988-89, scoring five goals from the left-back position. After some impressive displays in the early part of the season, injury forced him to miss the second half of the campaign.

During the summer of 1990, Hinchcliffe was transferred to Everton in exchange for Neil Pointon and a large cash adjustment in City's favour. He made his Everton debut at Goodison against Leeds United on the opening day of the 1990-91 season. Although injured early in the campaign, he recovered enough to play in 30 matches, including the losing Zenith Data Final against Crystal Palace.

Once regarded as one of the most promising left-backs in the country, Hinchcliffe was not highly regarded by Blues' manager Howard Kendall, hence his transfer from City. In 1991-92 he had a run in the team at left-back but, following the arrival of Gary Ablett, his only appearances were on the left-side of midfield. After this disappointment, he started the following season in his favoured left-back position but unfortunately he suffered yet another setback to his Everton career when a pelvic injury put him out of action for two months.

Hinchcliffe played on a more regular basis after that, using his speed and agility to make important defensive tackles. Extremely useful in dead ball situations where his curling shots caused keepers in the Premiership great headaches, it was his brilliant corner that set up the Blues' FA Cup semi-final win over Tottenham Hotspur. He ended the 1994-95 season with his first major honour in the game, following the Toffees[' great FA Cup Final victory against Manchester United.

He continued at left-back for Everton in 1995-96 until he lost his place to another gifted left-footer, David Unsworth and thereafter he spent much of his time on the bench. However, he bounced back the following season and was enjoying the most outstanding campaign of his career until sustaining cruciate ligament damage against Leeds United in December 1997.

During the course of the early part of the season, Hinchcliffe had been called up by England coach Glenn Hoddle to fill the left wing-back role in Moldova, a task he carried out so effectively that he retained his place in the side for the next two internationals. Unfortunately, his injury ruled him out of the World Cup qualifier against Italy.

Having spent seven months recuperating, Hinchcliffe finally returned against Derby County but was sent off for a professional foul. However, he soon picked where he left off and quickly reclaimed his England place too.

A well-publicised difference of opinion with manager Howard Kendall meant that few were surprised when he was transferred to Sheffield Wednesday for £2.85 million in January 1998.

Quickly settling in at Hillsborough, he scored against Liverpool in his third match and though the Owls were relegated in 1999-2000, there is no doubt that, injury free, Andy Hinchcliffe remains a class player.

Honours
FA Cup 1994-95
7 England Caps

JOHN HURST

Born	6 February 1947	
Birthplace	Blackpool	
Height	6ft 0 ins	
Weight	12 st 6 lbs	

Team	Apps	Gls
Everton	336 (1)	29
Oldham Ath.	169 (1)	2

A dedicated clubman, John Hurst arrived at Goodison in a blaze of publicity as a 14-year-old centre-forward who had starred for Blackpool and England schoolboys. Blues' manager Harry Catterick converted him into a defensive wing-half and after a series of outstanding displays during the club's 1965 FA Youth Cup triumph he made his League debut against Stoke City. Over the course of that 1965-66 season, Hurst not only provided cover for Jimmy Gabriel and Brian Harris but also deputised for England striker Fred Pickering. However, his most effective role was playing alongside Brian Labone at the heart of the Blues' defence.

Comfortable in possession, Hurst was an intelligent reader of the game and like most defenders relished getting forward, especially at set pieces. He

was also most adept at man-to-man marking and his immaculate policing of Roger Hunt in the 1-0 fifth round FA Cup victory over Liverpool in March 1967 confirmed his progress. On the eve of the club's FA Cup semi-final against Leeds United at Old Trafford in April 1968, Hurst went down with hepatitis. He confounded medical experts who told him he wouldn't play again that season by turning out for the Blues in the final against West Bromwich Albion.

Hurst was ever-present for the next two seasons, including the Blues' League Championship campaign of 1969-70 when his form led to him captaining England's Under-23 team. Hurst was most unlucky not to win full international honours but unfortunately for him, he was around at the same time as Bobby Moore, Norman Hunter and Colin Todd.

During the course of that 1969-70

season, Hurst scored a number of vital goals but perhaps none better than the cracking 25-yarder following a neat interchange with Alan Ball to sink Manchester United at Old Trafford and the smart close-range hook shot to secure the points against arch-rivals Arsenal at Highbury.

Possessing one of the coolest heads in the Football League, Hurst surprisingly lost his place in the Everton side as new manager Billy Bingham sought unsuccessfully to build a side capable of emulating the triumphs of the Catterick era.

In the summer of 1976 'Gentleman Jack', the quietest man in the Goodison Park dressing-room, moved to Oldham Athletic where, still one of soccer's most polished defenders, he spent five effective seasons as a Boundary Park regular. He was without doubt Jimmy Frizzell's best-ever bargain. He went on to appear in 170 Second Division games for the Latics before deciding to hang up his boots in 1981.

When Hurst returned to Goodison for a spell as the club's youth coach in the nineties, the Blues' youngsters couldn't have wished for a better role model.

Honours
League Championship
1969-70

JIMMY HUSBAND

Born	25 October 1947
Birthplace	Newcastle
Height	5ft 9 ins
Weight	11 st 2 lbs

Team	Apps	Gls
Everton	158 (7)	44
Luton Town	138(5)	44

Jimmy Husband was a likeable and talented Geordie who was nicknamed 'Skippy' by the Blues' supporters because of his distinctive style of running. He was signed from north-east side Shields in the summer of 1963 and after working his way up through the ranks, made his Football League debut as a 17-year-old at Fulham in April 1965.

Husband had joined the Blues as an inside-forward but found that his most effective role was wide on the right. Specialising in diagonal runs across the face of defences, he would drag opponents out of position with his teasing skill. Still only 17 when he played for Everton against Hungarian side Ujpest Dozsa in the 1965-66 Inter Cities Fairs Cup, he went on to become one of the most exciting in the country. Though there were many times when he was completely

"Husband was capable of winning a game almost single-handedly with a flash of genuine brilliance."

unorthodox and totally unpredictable, he was also capable of winning a game almost single-handedly and with a flash of genuine brilliance.

After establishing himself as a first-team regular, Husband won England Under-23 honours but despite being on the fringes for a couple of seasons, he never gained a full international cap. He was at his sharpest in successive FA Cup quarter-finals - giving the Blues a two-goal lead, which they lost, against Nottingham Forest in 1967 and another brace the following year in a 3-1 win over Leicester City.

Unfortunately, that campaign was not to end happily for him and though the Blues reached the FA Cup Final against West Bromwich Albion, Husband fluffed a free header with the goal at his mercy. The miss condemned Everton to extra time and though they had

next few seasons saw his form affected by injury too and after his first-team opportunities became more restricted, he moved to Luton Town in November 1973.

Husband was the final piece in Harry Haslam's promotion jigsaw, scoring eight goals in 22 games as the Hatters finished runners-up to Middlesbrough in the Second Division. Included in that total was a hat-trick in a 3-1 home win over Orient. Husband was a regular member of the Luton side for the next five seasons, topping the club's scoring charts in 1975-76 with 14 goals. His best goalscoring performance came in the 7-1 rout of Charlton Athletic in September 1977 when Husband scored four of Luton's goals.

On leaving the club at the end of that season, Husband severed all ties with the game, but in 1984 he was tempted out of retirement to play for a Bedfordshire village side. Their name? Everton!

outplayed the Baggies for much of the game, that Jeff Astle goal won their opponents the trophy.

Husband's best season in terms of goals scored was undoubtedly 1968-69 when, linking lethally with Joe Royle, he plundered 20 League and Cup goals. The following term he played an important role in the Blues' League Championship winning success, though he was forced to miss the last few games through injury. Sadly, the

Honours
League Championship
1969-70

TOMMY
E JONES

Born	11 April 1930
Birthplace	Liverpool
Height	5ft 11 ins
Weight	11 st 12 lbs

Team	Apps	Gls
Everton	383	14

Everton's first-choice centre-half throughout the 1950s, Tommy Jones joined the Blues after successfully captaining the England and Liverpool County FA Youth teams. Although for many years he was regarded as a stopper, he had joined the club as a full-back. It was Blues' manager Cliff Britton who converted him to the role of pivot when the club needed a long-term replacement for his namesake Thomas Gwynfor Jones in 1950-51.

Tommy E Jones made his Everton debut in a 2-1 defeat at Arsenal and though he was much more basic in style than his predecessor he reigned supreme at the heart of the Blues' defence for the rest of the decade.

Tall and commanding, he invariably excelled in clashes with Bolton Wanderers and England centre-forward Nat Lofthouse and there were a number of occasions when not only the 'Lion of Vienna' failed to score but none of his team-mates did either.

Though Jones was without doubt one of the most consistent centre-halfs in the top flight, he did perhaps lack the streak of ruthlessness that runs through most top-level defenders. Cool, unruffled and a most gentlemanly player, Jones found the idea of stooping to foul methods to stop his opponent quite inconceivable.

Though most of his goals for Everton came through his ability to convert penalties, he did manage to score two with his head in the 4-2 defeat of Manchester United in October 1954 as the Blues sought to consolidate in Division One after their promotion the previous season. During the club's promotion-winning campaign of 1953-54, the player was outstanding. It was no coincidence that in one of the few matches he missed through injury, the Blues were beaten 5-1 by Birmingham City. Jones' only goal that season was the final one of the campaign as Everton beat Oldham Athletic 4-0.

When Peter Farrell left Goodison to become player-manager of Tranmere Rovers, Jones became Everton captain. However, shortly afterwards his slowness on the turn which had always been slightly in evidence grew more marked and in September 1958

Arsenal's Scottish international forward David Herd gave him a fearful chasing at Goodison, scoring four times in a 6-1 win for the Gunners. This led to Jones being replaced by the promising Brian Labone. Though he then found himself in the club's Central League side, he was not finished, reverting to left-back and winning back his place in the side.

Although full international honours surprisingly passed him by, Jones played for an England XI against the Army at Maine Road and was captain of the FA side that toured Ghana and Nigeria in the summer of 1958.

Sadly, a smashed kneecap in a Central League game at Barnsley forced him to retire and when Jones left Goodison to coach Italian League club Montreal, the Blues bade farewell to one of their most loyal players.

Uncertain Beginnings

Very few people outside Merseyside realise that had it not been for a rift in Everton FC in 1892, Liverpool FC would never have existed. A rent dispute at Anfield Road (yes, the very ground that Liverpool use today) caused a core of Everton players and members to look elsewhere for a ground. They chose Goodison Park while the remaining club was forced by the League to change their name from Everton Athletic Grounds Ltd to Liverpool because they did not want two clubs with the name Everton. The rest is, as they say, history!

Here are some more interesting facts about the relationship between the clubs:
* Liverpool still play on Everton's old ground, Anfield. Although the surrounding stands bear no relation to the Anfield that Everton occupied, Liverpool still play on the same pitch. It is still in the same location.
* Everton won their first championship at Anfield.
* Everton hosted an international between England and Ireland at Anfield, it was considered so good at the time.
* The largest audience to ever watch a Derby game at Everton was 78,299 in September 1948 which is also Everton's biggest attendance in history.

HOWARD KENDALL

Born	22 May 1946
Birthplace	Ryton-on-Tyne
Height	5ft 10 ins
Weight	11 st 4 lbs

Team	Apps	Gls
Preston NE	104	13
Everton	231 (2)	21
Birmingham C	115	16
Stoke City	82	9
Blackburn R	79	0

Howard Kendall was the youngest player ever to appear in an FA Cup Final when, at the age of 17 years 345 days, he played for Preston North End against West Ham United in 1964. During 1964-65, Kendall was chosen for an FA team under Alf Ramsey that made a two-match tour of Gibraltar. The side won both games, Kendall scoring in both of them.

In March 1967, Everton manager Harry Catterick paid North End £80,000 for the 21-year-old and two days after putting pen to paper, he made his debut for the Toffees against Southampton. He went on to be part of one of the most influential midfield combinations that Everton have ever had. Along with Alan Ball and Colin Harvey he helped the Blues to an emphatic League Championship success in 1969-70.

A wing-half from the old school, Kendall was a steady passer, defended well and made good forward runs, but he didn't score many goals. He collected Football League representative honours and Under-23 caps and was unlucky not to have got into the senior side. He was good enough to have played for England, for at times his influence in midfield at Everton was quite awesome.

In February 1974 he was part of a complex transfer package that took Bob Latchford from Birmingham City to Everton while Kendall made the opposite journey. He proved a reliable buy for the St Andrew's club, helping to stabilise them in the First Division and also taking them to the 1975 FA Cup semi-finals.

In August 1977 he joined Stoke City for £40,000 and became the club coach under Alan Durban as Stoke won promotion to Division One in 1978-79.

In the close season he arrived at Blackburn Rovers as the club's player-manager. During his time at Ewood, it was his performances on the field as much as anything else that helped take the club from the Third Division to the brink of the First Division within two seasons. Despite entering the veteran stage of his career, he showed all he determination and drive of his earlier days, dictating play and inspiring those around him.

It was perhaps the least surprising event in his career when in the summer of 1981 he returned to Goodison as player-manager. He had his problems in those early days, but in 1983-84 the club won the FA Cup and reached the final of the League Cup. The following season, Everton won the League Championship and the European Cup Winners' Cup as well as reaching the FA Cup Final. Kendall was named Manager of the Year.

After winning the League Championship in 1986-87, Kendall felt he could do no more and was enticed to Athletico Bilbao in Spain. He has since managed Manchester City, Everton again, Notts County, Sheffield United and Everton for a third time, parting company with the club following a season in which they hung on to their Premiership status on goal difference from Bolton Wanderers.

Honours
League Championship
1969-70

ANDY KING

Born	14 August 1956	
Birthplace	Luton	
Height	5ft 9 ins	
Weight	11 st 0 lbs	

Team	Apps	Gls
Luton Town	33 (3)	9
Everton	193 (2)	49
QPR	28 (2)	9
West Brom	21 (4)	9
Wolves	28	10
Aldershot	36	11

A former Spurs schoolboy, Andy King worked his way up through the ranks at Luton Town before making his Football League debut for his home-town club as a substitute in a 1-1 draw against Manchester City on the final day of the 1974-75 season. After winning a regular place the following season, he looked to have a successful career ahead of him with the Hatters but he became an Evertonian when Blues' manager and former Luton player Billy Bingham paid £35,000 for his services in April 1976.

King made an immediate impression with three live-wire displays that inspired victories and won the approval of his team-mates, who had been promised a Spanish holiday if they picked up at least four points from the final three games of the season. In one of those games, King scored twice and hit the woodwork in a 3-1 win at Derby County. After that, he became a fixture in the Everton side; his control, distribution and finishing winning him England Under-21 recognition.

King confirmed his stature by scoring one of the most welcome goals in the club's history in October 1978: firing home a 20-yard volley past Liverpool's England international 'keeper Ray Clemence, he ended the Reds' seven-year domination of Merseyside derby games.

Shortly afterwards, however, his form became patchy and new manager Gordon Lee, who made no secret of his preference for solidity over wayward brilliance, decided to part company with King - an individual who exuded the sheer joy of football.

> *"King scored one of the most welcome goals in Everton's history: firing home a 20-yard volley past Ray Clemence, to end the Reds' seven-year domination of derby games."*

In September 1980, King joined Queen's Park Rangers for £450,000 but after just one year at Loftus Road, he moved to West Bromwich Albion for a similar fee.

In the summer of 1982, Everton boss Howard Kendall dispatched Peter Eastoe to West Bromwich Albion in exchange for Andy King in the hope that the formerly erratic midfielder had matured and could begin to harness his undoubted talent. He certainly started impressively, scoring with a sensational 25-yard curler in the 5-0 demolition of Aston Villa. Unfortunately, his progress was hampered by a serious knee injury suffered in a 2-1 defeat at Sunderland and afterwards he found it difficult to hold down a place in an Everton side that was improving rapidly. Dismayed at being an outsider, King was allowed to leave and join Dutch club Cambuur. He later returned to England to play for Wolves before spending another spell, albeit a brief one, with Luton. He ended his playing career with Aldershot.

On retiring, King ran a soccer school on Merseyside, then rejoined Luton as the Kenilworth Road club's commercial manager. He later entered management with Mansfield Town. Though he won no caps or medals, Andy King played the game with a flair and vision that endeared him to the fans, even during those frustratingly inconsistent spells that punctuated his career.

BRIAN LABONE

Born	23 January 1940
Birthplace	Liverpool
Height	6ft 1 ins
Weight	12 st 11 lbs

Team	Apps	Gls
Everton	451	2

One of the greatest players to wear the royal blue of Everton, Brian Labone won every honour in the game, including 26 England caps and he captained the club for seven years. Labone made his Everton debut at the age of 18 in March 1958 when the Blues' regular centre-half Tommy Jones was injured. On his first appearance at Goodison Park, he was given a chasing by Spurs' Bobby Smith as the Blues lost 4-3 and, with the young Labone responsible for three of the goals, he was dropped.

Recalled midway through the following season, Labone went on to become one of the game's great competitors. He was only booked twice in 530 first team appearances, playing against some of the game's roughest and toughest strikers in the country. He later found that strikers became much more subtle as the old formation was replaced by 4-2-4. Everton now operated with two centre-backs and this was the time that John Hurst joined him at the heart of the Blues' defence.

Labone won the first of his 26 England caps in October 1962, playing against Northern Ireland in Belfast. He was only 22-years-old and was the first Everton player since the war to be capped - a great achievement. In 1966 he had a chance of being England's World Cup centre-half but he made a shock request to be overlooked in order that he could go ahead with his planned summer marriage to a former Miss Liverpool. That news soon took a back seat as Labone fulfilled his boyhood dream and led the Blues to victory in the FA Cup Final against Sheffield Wednesday.

Just sixteen months after that

be staying on to allow Everton to use his ability and experience to the full in a team of very promising youngsters. He was a key figure when the League Championship returned to Goodison in 1970.

One of the greatest of clubmen, Labone was a pillar in the Everton defence for fifteen seasons. It was reckoned that there was no safer sight in football than Brian Labone marshalling his defenders. A great leader, he captained a Football League XI against the Irish and led an FA select side in Canada.

Brian Labone was of the old school, surviving in the football revolution to remain the model professional. He finished his career on 24 August 1971, just twelve games short of Ted Sagar's all-time Everton record. Forced to quit the game after an Achilles tendon injury, Labone's loss was a shattering blow to Everton and one that they would feel for the next decade.

Wembley success, he dropped a bombshell by announcing his retirement. He revealed that he wasn't enjoying his football and would be quitting at the end of his contract or earlier if Everton could find a suitable replacement. Having made this announcement, Labone began to produce some of his best-ever football and was recalled into the England squad. Some sixteen months later, he announced he would

BOB LATCHFORD

Born	18 January 1951	
Birthplace	Birmingham	
Height	6ft 1 ins	
Weight	12 st 11 lbs	

Team	Apps	Gls
Birmingham C	158 (2)	68
Everton	235 (1)	106
Swansea C	87	35
Coventry C	11 (1)	2
Lincoln City	14 (1)	2
Newport Co.	20	5

Bob Latchford began his Football League career with Birmingham City, scoring twice on his debut in a 3-2 win over Preston North End in March 1969. After five years at St Andrew's, in which Latchford scored 84 goals in 194 games, Everton manager Billy Bingham paid a record fee of £350,000 for the Birmingham centre-forward with Howard Kendall and Archie Styles going in the opposite direction.

Latchford took a little time to settle at Goodison Park but once he did, the goals started to flow.

A strong, burly centre-forward, he was a difficult man to shake off the ball and was strong in the air. He had the special knack of turning half chances into goals and was Everton's leading scorer for four consecutive seasons from 1975.

"Latchford had the special knack of turning half chances into goals and was Everton's leading scorer for four consecutive seasons from 1975."

At the outset of the 1977-78 campaign, the Daily Express announced that it would award £10,000 to the first player in the top two divisions of the Football League to reach thirty goals. In October of that season Latchford scored four when Everton beat Queen's Park Rangers 5-1 at Loftus Road. He also netted a hat trick in a 6-0 home victory over Coventry City with winger Dave Thomas providing the crosses. On 29 April 1978 in a 6-0 thrashing of Chelsea, Latchford scored the two goals he needed to become the first top-flight player for six years to score thirty. It was a close call, for there were only eight minutes of the season left. However, Latchford didn't receive anywhere near £10,000 - just £192 to be exact. It was part of the deal that £5,000 went to the Football

League and Professional Footballers' Association Benevolent Fund and Bob generously shared the remainder between all the players who had helped him to achieve his thirty-goal haul.

Also that season, Latchford made his full England debut in a World Cup qualifying match against Italy at Wembley. He appeared twelve times for his country, only playing on the losing side in his last match against Austria.

During the course of the 1978-79 season, he scored a stunning five goals as Everton trounced Wimbledon in a League Cup match. He remained at Goodison for a further three seasons after that memorable thirty goal campaign, taking his tally of goals to 138 in 289 League and Cup games - the club's leading goalscorer since the war.

When Howard Kendall returned to Everton as player-manager, Latchford was the first player to depart, joining Swansea City. He enjoyed mixed fortunes in South Wales but he did score 32 goals in 1982-83 before being given a free transfer and joining Dutch club Breda. Within five months he had returned to these shores and signed for Coventry City, leaving twelve months later to play for Lincoln City before ending his League career with Newport County.

Honours
12 England caps

GARY LINEKER

Born	30 November 1960	
Birthplace	Leicester	
Height	5ft 11 ins	
Weight	12 st 2 lbs	

Team	Apps	Gls
Leicester City	187 (7)	95
Everton	41	30
Tottenham H	105	67

A member of Leicester City's 1980 Second Division Championship winning team, earning promotion again in 1983, Gary Lineker's great asset in his early days was his blistering pace and he top-scored for four successive seasons at Filbert Street. With 103 League and Cup goals for Leicester, a move was inevitable.

Lineker arrived on Merseyside in the summer of 1985 after protracted negotiations between Blues' boss Howard Kendall and the Leicester board had threatened to break down on a number of occasions. Everton valued Lineker at £400,000 while the Foxes wanted £1.25 million - the eventual fee of £800,000 plus a percentage of any future fee was set by an independent tribunal.

Though he failed to find the net on his first three appearances, Lineker soon struck up a superb attacking partnership with Graeme Sharp. He went on to score 38 goals in 52 outings, including three hat-tricks in wins over Birmingham City (home 4-1), Manchester City (home 4-0) and Southampton (home 6-1). He tormented defences the length and breadth of the League and as the season neared its climax the Blues looked a reasonable bet to clinch the League and FA Cup double.

Lineker's contribution was recognised by awards from the PFA and Football Writers' Association who both voted him their Player of the Year. Sadly his efforts were unrewarded in terms of tangible success as the Blues finished runners-up in both the League and FA Cup, although he did score the opening goal of the historic all-Merseyside FA Cup Final.

Along with team-mates Peter Reid, Trevor Steven and Gary Stevens, Lineker was a key figure in England's 1986 World Cup campaign and ended it as the leading scorer in the finals with six goals.

Lineker travelled back from Mexico amid mounting speculation that he would soon be sold to the highest

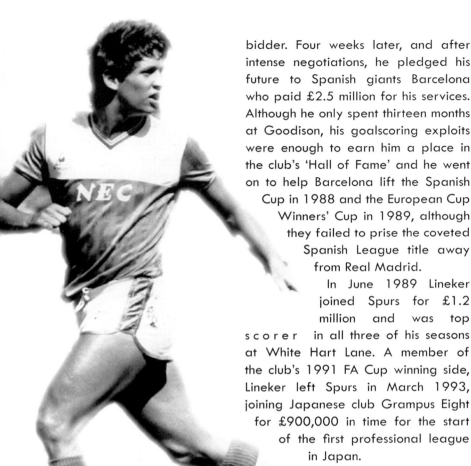

bidder. Four weeks later, and after intense negotiations, he pledged his future to Spanish giants Barcelona who paid £2.5 million for his services. Although he only spent thirteen months at Goodison, his goalscoring exploits were enough to earn him a place in the club's 'Hall of Fame' and he went on to help Barcelona lift the Spanish Cup in 1988 and the European Cup Winners' Cup in 1989, although they failed to prise the coveted Spanish League title away from Real Madrid.

In June 1989 Lineker joined Spurs for £1.2 million and was top scorer in all three of his seasons at White Hart Lane. A member of the club's 1991 FA Cup winning side, Lineker left Spurs in March 1993, joining Japanese club Grampus Eight for £900,000 in time for the start of the first professional league in Japan.

At international level, Lineker was desperately unlucky not to surpass Bobby Charlton's record of 49 goals, falling just one goal short of equalling the Manchester United player's record. Never booked during his entire career, his services to football were rewarded in the 1992 New Year's Honours List with the OBE.

Still a thoroughly approachable and likeable individual, Gary Lineker has created a new career as a television personality.

**Honours
80 England caps**

MICK LYONS

Born	8 December 1951
Birthplace	Liverpool
Height	6ft 0 ins
Weight	12 st 0 lbs

Team	Apps	Gls
Everton	364 (25)	48
Sheffield Wed	129	12
Grimsby Town	50	4

A player who once admitted that he would readily run through a brick wall to further the Everton cause, Mick Lyons spent many of his boyhood Saturdays on the Goodison terraces. After rising through the junior ranks to the club's reserve side as a teenage striker, he was reduced to 'A' team status by the progress of David Johnson. This prompted his conversion to central defender and after a series of impressive displays in the Central League he made his senior debut at Nottingham Forest in 1971.

There then followed two in-and-out seasons before he established himself as a regular at the heart of the Blues' defence. Though for the most part he was content with halting opposition forwards, Lyons could be a potent attacking force too. Everton managers Billy Bingham and Gordon Lee both selected him for emergency spells at centre-forward, while if the Blues were losing he would move up front for the last few minutes of a game. In 1973-

74 he was the club's top scorer with 1 League and Cup goals, testimony to hi versatility.

It was around this time that h won international recognition, bein selected for England at Under-23 an 'B' level. He was also made captain o his beloved Everton.

Throughout his Everton caree Lyons was never on the winning sid in a derby match, missing the onl two victories achieved by the Blue in this period. Against Liverpool i December 1973 he found the ne with a majestic header only to hav the 'goal' disallowed and even mor excruciating, he volleyed a 40-yar own goal past a dumbfounded Georg Wood in a 2-2 draw at Anfield almo: six years later. Following that inciden a surprisingly joyful Everton supporte approached him in a local pub, sayin that he'd drawn Mick's name in sweep as the scorer of the first goc and had won £40.

Lyons captained the Blues to th

1977 League Cup Final, in which he scored in the second replay but it wasn't enough to secure victory over Aston Villa - it was the nearest he came to winning a trophy in his time at Goodison.

Early in 1982 at the age of thirty, he lost his regular place in the side when Billy Wright was brought into Howard Kendall's constantly changing side to partner Mark Higgins. After waiting patiently for a recall that never came, Lyons severed his ties with the club in August that year, joining Sheffield Wednesday. A natural choice as captain, he led the Owls to the FA Cup semi-finals in 1982-83 and the following season was an ever-present as the club finally won promotion back to the First Division.

In November 1985, Lyons became Grimsby Town's player-coach but was sacked in June 1987 after they were relegated. A month later he rejoined Everton as reserve team coach. Dismissed following the appointment of Howard Kendall, he was appointed first team coach at Wigan Athletic and then Huddersfield Town. He later accepted a post of coach to the Brunei national team.

JOHNNY MORRISSEY

Born	18 April 1940
Birthplace	Liverpool
Height	5ft 9ins
Weight	11st 12lbs

Team	Apps	Gls
Liverpool	36	6
Everton	257 (2)	43
Oldham Ath.	6	1

Johnny Morrissey began his career with Liverpool but in September 1962 he moved across Stanley Park to Goodison for a fee of £10,000. The transfer had been sanctioned by the Liverpool board but without the agreement of manager Bill Shankly. He made it quite clear than any further transactions without his blessing would result in his departure from Anfield!

Morrissey's early displays for the Blues certainly seemed to strengthen Shanks' case for, after coming close on a number of occasions, the Everton winger opened his account in the Merseyside derby as the Blues drew 2-2 against their arch-rivals. The following week, Morrissey netted a hat-trick in a 4-2 home win over West Bromwich Albion, going on to help Everton win the League Championship in his first season with the club.

> "Morrissey was the 'Pocket Hercules' of a side that won national acclaim for its cultured football in 1969-70."

Despite this success, Morrissey foun that he had to share the No.11 shi with Derek Temple and indeed misse out on FA Cup glory in 1966 whe the Blues beat Sheffield Wednesda 3-2. Determined to claim a regulo first-team spot, Morrissey hit the be form of his career as the decad came to a close. He was the man wh guaranteed Everton a plac in the 1968 FA Cup Fin with a dramatic penalt winner against higl flying Leeds United i the semi-final at Ol Trafford. The tenaciou and gutsy winger place the spot-kick wide of Wels international keeper Gary Sprak to set up a Wembley showdown wit West Bromwich Albion, a match th Blues lost 1-0.

Morrissey's ball control with eithe foot was impeccable while h intelligent assessment of attackin situations proved the downfall c

mercilessly tormented the Yorkshire club's right-back Paul Reaney in an outstanding display of wing play. Though the Blues had a disappointing season in 1970-71, Morrissey continued to torment the top flight's best defenders, laying on the majority of Joe Royle's goals. Yet the following season he found it difficult to hold down a regular first-team place and in the close season he was transferred to

many of Everton's opponents. Hugging the touchline, he was explosively quick over very short distances and, although he occasionally cut inside to hit a powerful shot with his right foot, he was at his best when tricking his way to the by-line and floating over one of his devastatingly accurate crosses.

Morrissey was the 'Pocket Hercules' of a side that won national acclaim for its cultured football in 1969-70, earning Johnny a second League Championship medal. When Everton beat the reigning champions Leeds United 3-2, Morrissey

Oldham Athletic. Sadly it wasn't too long before injury ended his career.

One of the shrewdest buys the Blues have ever made, Johnny Morrissey is now a successful businessman. He retained an interest in the game through the progress of his son, also John, who, after two appearances for Everton, carved out an admirable career for himself with Tranmere Rovers.

Honours
League Championship
1962-63, 1969-70

PAT NEVIN

Born	6 September 1963
Birthplace	Glasgow
Height	5ft 6ins
Weight	11st 9lbs

Team	Apps	Gls
Chelsea	190 (3)	36
Everton	81 (28)	16
Tranmere R	189 (12)	30

One of the few players of modern times who could justifiably claim to have natural balance and grace of movement, Pat Nevin played his early football for Clyde in the Scottish League before joining Chelsea in May 1983 for a fee of £95,000. In his first season at Stamford Bridge, he helped the London club win the Second Division Championship, contributing 14 vital goals.

Nevin maintained his high standards in the top flight the following season, his looping, curling crosses providing Kerry Dixon and David Speedie with a steady stream of chances. He won his first Scottish cap against Romania in March 1986 but, as Chelsea lost their way, he saw less of the ball and was usually closely marked by two or three men. Following defeat at the hands of Middlesbrough

> "One of the few players of modern times who could justifiably claim to have natural balance and grace of movement,"

in the play-offs in May 1988, Nevin exercised his right to move on and joined Everton, a transfer tribunal setting the fee at £925,000 after bitter wrangling.

The thoughtful Scot, a devotee of obscure rock bands and Russian literature, made his Everton debut in a 4-0 home win over Newcastle United on the opening day of the 1988-89 season. His ability to leave defenders trailing in his wake ensured that he was quickly accepted by the discerning Everton supporters and this was never more in evidence than in October 1989 when he went round three Arsenal defenders and goalkeeper Lukic before netting with panache in a 3-0 win over the Gunners. Similarly, his touch and vision were never better seen than in the Merseyside derby a month earlier. With a sudden outside-of-the-foot backspin chip, he paralysed the Reds' defence before crossing for Mike Newell to beat Grobbelaar. However, Liverpool ran out winners 3-1.

Perhaps Nevin's finest moment in an Everton shirt came in the FA Cup semi-final in 1989 when he scored the goal to beat Norwich City. Sadly, his joy was totally overshadowed by the tragic events which had unfolded in the other semi-final at Hillsborough that same afternoon.

His form in 1990-91 was so persuasive that he not only won a recall to the Scotland side but missed only one league match. The return of Howard Kendall to the club failed to bring about a change of fortune, and with Ward, Warzycha and Beagrie all in contention for a first-team place, the wee Scot was placed on the transfer list at his own request.

After moving across the Mersey to play for Tranmere Rovers, Nevin missed very few games in his five seasons with the Prenton Park club. He continued to be selected for Scotland, winning 14 caps while with Rovers. Though not a prolific scorer, he netted a hat-trick in a 5-1 League Cup win over Oxford United in September 1993.

The PFA Chairman, Pat Nevin was a great ambassador for Tranmere Rovers, leaving the club to play for

Kllmarnock, who he helped to fourth place in the Scottish Premier League in 1997-98.

Honours
28 Scotland caps

FRED PICKERING

Born	19 January 1941
Birthplace	Blackburn
Height	5ft 11ins
Weight	12st 8lbs

Team	Apps	Gls
Blackburn R	134	61
Everton	97	56
Birmingham City	74	27
Blackpool	48 (1)	24

One of Everton's finest post-war strikers, Fred Pickering began his career as a full-back with Blackburn Rovers. He had enjoyed success in the Rovers' junior teams, helping to win the FA Youth Cup in 1959, but when given a first-team chance he failed to make a lasting impression.

Rovers' manager Jack Marshall decided to gamble with him at centre-forward after some powerful displays playing in that position in the reserves. Despite his initial clumsy approach work, Pickering had the happy knack of putting the ball in the net and was soon to make quite a name for himself. He had begun to add pace and power to his game and played havoc with the best defences in the land.

However, after 123 league games and 59 goals, Pickering became unsettled and wanted a transfer. Blackburn were in their best league position for years but incredibly and controversially, the club let him go.

A then British record fee of £85,000 took him to Everton in what was to prove a wise signing, as the tall dashing centre-forward threatened defences throughout the First Division. Pickering began well, scoring a hat-trick on his home debut as the Blues beat Nottingham Forest 6-1, yet it during the final few games of that season that Everton lost the title - Pickering possibly upsetting the balance and rhythm of the side. However, he still netted nine goals in nine matches.

Two months later, in his first match for England, he scored another hat-trick as the United States were beaten 10-0. In 1964-65 he proved to be worth every penny of his huge transfer fee collecting 27 goals including a hat-trick during a 4-1 home win over Tottenham Hotspur.

Pickering remained in splendid form the following season but in March 1966, in the Merseyside derby, he twisted and his leg collapsed under him. After missing a couple of games he returned, only for the leg to go again against Sheffield United when

he went up for a high ball and came down on his knee. He had to miss the FA Cup semi-final and the final against Sheffield Wednesday.

Popular with the Everton fans, with fewer injuries and a different temperament, he could have become one of the really great Everton footballers. In August 1967 he moved to Birmingham City, proving to be a prolific marksman for the Midlands club. He returned to the north-west in 1969, signing for Blackpool and, after helping the Seasiders win promotion to the First Division, he returned to Blackburn Rovers in March 1971. Cast in the role of saviour as Rovers faced Third Division football for the first time in their history, he was released the following season after manager Ken Furphy claimed he was out of condition. Later he attempted to revive his career with Brighton and Hove Albion but without much success.

Honours
3 England caps

KEVIN RATCLIFFE

	Born	12 November 1960
	Birthplace	Mancot
	Height	6ft 0ins
	Weight	13st 6lbs

Team	Apps	Gls
Everton	356 (3)	2
Cardiff City	25	1
Derby County	6	0
Chester City	23	0

The most successful captain in the history of Everton Football Club, Kevin Ratcliffe played in the same Flintshire Schools' side as Ian Rush. On completion of his education, a host of top sides offered him apprenticeship forms but there was only one club that interested him and he duly signed for his beloved Everton for on the rare occasions he was not kicking a ball about as a boy, he could be found cheering on the likes of Ball and Royle from the Goodison terraces.

Ratcliffe signed professional forms in the summer of 1978 and after kicking his heels in the Blues' Central League side for two years, he made his League debut against Manchester United in March 1980. He played in one other game that season but did enough to earn both an Under-21 call-up and a first-team place by the start of the 1980-81 season.

In November 1980 Ratcliffe made his full international debut for Wales against Czechoslovakia, marking dangerman Masny out of the game.

Many of his early games for Everton were at left-back and, upset at being played out of position, he went to confront the Blues' new manager Howard Kendall. At one stage there was even talk of a move to Ipswich Town when Bobby Robson showed an interest, but thankfully he remained at Goodison Park.

In December 1982, Ratcliffe's fortunes took a decisive upturn when he replaced the overweight Billy Wright alongside Mark Higgins at the heart of the Everton defence. Within twelve months he had succeeded the injury-ravaged Higgins as captain and the following March he was leading his country. In March 1984 at the age of 23, Ratcliffe became the youngest man since Bobby Moore some twenty years earlier to lift the FA Cup. Within the next year he had led his team forward to pick up the FA Charity Shield, the League Championship and the European Cup Winners' Cup

Thereafter he skippered the Blues to the runners-up spot in both the League and the FA up in 1985-86 and to another League title in 1986-87.

Ratcliffe's role at Everton was crucial as the Blues' game was built on a very sound defensive system. They often played a tight and rigid offside game but, if a striker did break through, Ratcliffe's speed was such that the danger was snuffed out immediately. Strong in the tackle, he possessed quite a ruthless streak that meant he couldn't be intimidated.

Despite losing some of his astonishing speed following a serious groin injury which plagued him for a couple of seasons, he continued to retain the style and consistency that made him one of the world's classiest defenders. After losing his place to Martin Keown, Ratcliffe was placed on the transfer list and in the spring of 1992 he joined Cardiff City, helping them win promotion to the 'new' Second Division. After a spell managing Chester City, he then took charge of Shrewsbury Town.

Honours
League Championship
1984-85, 1986-87
FA Cup 1983-84
European Cup Winners' Cup
1984-85
59 Wales caps

PETER REID

Born	20 June 1956
Birthplace	Huyton
Height	5ft 8ins
Weight	10st 8lbs

Team	Apps	Gls
Bolton W	222 (3)	23
Everton	155 (4)	8
Q.P.R.	29	1
Man City	90 (13)	1
Southampton	7	0
Notts County	5	0
Bury	1	0
Darlington	1	0

Peter Reid played schoolboy football for Huyton Boys, a side that caused something of an upset when they won the English Schools Trophy in 1970. Many scouts came to the games and the chance came for Reid to join various clubs as an apprentice. He opted for Bolton Wanderers and made his debut as a substitute against Orient in October 1974.

Reid soon established himself in the Bolton side and was ever-present for the next two seasons as the Wanderers just missed out on promotion. His cultured midfield play and his intense desire to be involved all the time were features of Bolton's Second Division Championship winning side of 1977-78. Injury struck in a pre-season game and Reid missed Bolton's return to the top flight. He recovered to win back his midfield spot but again suffered the misfortune of a broken leg. On New Year's Day 1979, he collided with Everton goalkeeper George Wood on a snowbound Burnden Park pitch (the game was later abandoned). This time Reid was missing for a year.

Contractual problems prevented Reid from playing after he failed to agree terms with Arsenal, Wolves and Everton, all of whom offered £600,000 for his signature. Eventually he was placed on a weekly contract but in September 1981 he broke his leg yet again at Barnsley. The midfield star again won his battle for fitness, realising his ambition to get back into the top flight when he signed for Everton. It proved to be one of the Blues' most significant post-war signings, although he wasn't an immediate success at Everton, playing just seven league games from the New Year.

At the end of the 1984-85 season, his most injury-free term, Everton won the League Championship and European Cup Winners' Cup and Reid was chosen by the Professional

Championship medals, an FA Cup winners' medal and a European Cup Winners' Cup medal along with 13 England caps, the first as a substitute against Mexico in 1985.

In 1987-88 Reid was appointed player-coach at Everton before being transferred to Queen's Park Rangers in 1989. After a short stay at Loftus Road, he returned to the north-west as Manchester City's player-coach. After Howard Kendall's unexpected return to Everton, Reid was the players and supporters choice to replace him. In his first season in charge, he led City to fifth place in the First Division, their highest league finish since 1978.

Reid then moved on to manage Sunderland, guiding the Black Cats into the Premier League as runaway First Division champions and later to seventh place in the Premiership in 2000-01 - their highest position in forty-five years. He was sacked in October 2002 following a string of poor results.

Footballers' Association as their Player of the Year.

Reid was the inspiration behind Everton's revival, powerfully initiating attacks while blocking and threatening the skills of the opposition. At Goodison Park he won two League

Honours
League Championship
1984-85, 1986-87
FA Cup 1983-84
European Cup Winners' Cup
1984-85
13 England caps

WAYNE ROONEY

Born	October 24th 1985
Birthplace	Liverpool
Height	5ft 10ins
Weight	11st 8lbs

Team	Apps	Gls
Everton	14 (19)	6

Teenage sensation Wayne Rooney burst onto the national stage in October 2002 following a 10-minute cameo appearance against unbeaten Premiership Champions Arsenal. The 16 year-old, still on amateur forms, came on as a substitute for Tomasz Radsinski in the 81st minute, with the game deadlocked at 1-1 and within minutes he had beaten England number one David Seaman with a wicked, dipping, swerving drive from 25 yards. The celebrations that ensued communicated the relief and joy of the Blues supporters as they recognised a 24-carat superhero and a devoted Evertonian to boot. In the Blues' following match, against Leeds at Elland Road, Wayne was on target again scoring the game's only goal - this time a meandering run from the half-way line capped by a cool finish from just inside the penalty area - again the travelling Evertonians went ballistic as if their prayers for a star of the future had finally been answered. Wayne went onto be pivotal to Everton's revival during the 2002-03 season.

Just 6 months previously Rooney had played an important role in Everton's run to the 2002 FA Youth Cup Final scoring 8 goals in 8 games and by the start of the 2002-03 season rumours of the lad' talent flooded the Everton grapevine. Ye the Croxteth-born youngster was still an unknown when he scored a wonder goal in an FA Youth Cup-tie at Tottenham that had Glenn Hoddle and David Pleat turning to Everton officials and asking, 'Who is this kid?'

From his debut in August 2002 against Tottenham at Goodison, during which he set up the opening goal for Mark Pembridge, Rooney dominated Evertonian thoughts and, following his immediate conversion into 'Roonaldo' in the wake of his single-handed demolition of Arsenal and Leeds, he became a symbol of hope for the entire nation and there were soon calls for his inclusion in the full England team. Wayne was subsequently voted BBC Young Sports Personality of the Year 2002.

Almost inevitably, Rooney became England's youngest-ever player, aged 17 years and 111 days, when he made his international debut against Australia on 12th February 2003 - his first touch being a delightful exchange of passes with Newcastle United's 2003 PFA Young Player of the Year Jermaine Jenas. This was followed by an appearance as substitute against Liechtenstein in a 2-0 England win. Yet controversy preceded

substitute against Liechtenstein in a 2-0 England win. Yet controversy preceeded the national side's Euro qualifier against Turkey, with many claiming that Wayne was too inexperienced to face a team that finished fourth in the 2002 World Cup. However Errriksson's brave decision to play the youngster ahead of Liverpool's Emile Heskey was fully justified with a glorious display that raised England's game to new heights.

Rooney, at 17 years 160 days England's youngest full debutant soon confirmed his talent and those present sensed they were witnessing the birth of a phenomenon. After a quiet start he took the game by the scruff of the neck, making two trademark runs that sparked a great England performacnce and contributed much to England's eventual 2-0 triumph - his dream debut was completed with a nomination as man of the match.

To put Rooney's talent in perspective, pundits have already likened Wayne's slaloming dribbling style to greats like Roberto Baggio and Paul Gascoigne, while old pros insist that his awareness, for a lad his age, is exceptional - a claim backed up by his performance against the Turks. The main fear for Evertonians must be that he avoids wearing himself out at too young an age. David Moyes has already admitted that protecting his protege will be one of his most important tasks over the next few seasons.

Yet, perhaps Everton chairman Bill Kenwright put it best when he called on everyone - from club to country - to 'cherish' the lad's talent.

Still, if Rooney goes on improving, and is capable of entering this list of the greatest Evertonians on the basis of just one season's work, few doubt that he will become a vital member of Everton teams of the future. He could be the greatest Evertonian of all-time.

JOE ROYLE

Born	8 April 1949
Birthplace	Liverpool
Height	6ft 1ins
Weight	12st 6lbs

Team	Apps	Gls
Everton	229 (3)	102
Man City	98 (1)	23
Bristol City	100 (1)	18
Norwich City	40 (2)	9

Even though he was brought up within a stone's throw of Goodison, Joe Royle used to watch Manchester United as often as he could! If he had followed his father's trade, he would have entertained crowds in a far different way, for Joe's father was a musician with a local trio.

Royle made his debut for Everton against Blackpool in January 1966, at the tender age of 16 years 282 days, becoming the youngest-ever player to represent the Blues until his record was beaten by Wayne Rooney in 2002-03. Royle came in for Alex Young and even at that age, he was stocky and powerful and had all the energy, confidence and skill of youth. It was after this game - Everton were beaten 2-0 - that manager Harry Catterick was attacked by the fans. Young Joe made only one more first-team appearance that season

at Leeds as the Blues were beaten again, this time 4-1.

The 1966-67 season was almost at an end before Joe Royle was again given his chance. He grabbed it - hitting two goals in a 3-1 win over Chelsea at Goodison. That was the first time he had appeared before his own fans for the league side. It was a display that banished the bitter Blackpool memory. He played in four games towards the end of the campaign, netting three goals.

Within four years, Royle had packed a wealth of experience into his sizeable frame and earned himself the reputation as one of Everton's finest post-war strikers and a fitting successor to the traditions of Dixie Dean and Tommy Lawton. He was a centre-forward with honest-to-goodness ideas about what his job demanded - the scoring of goals!

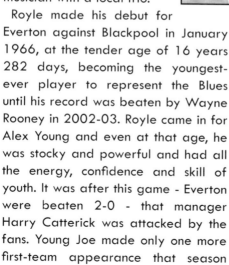

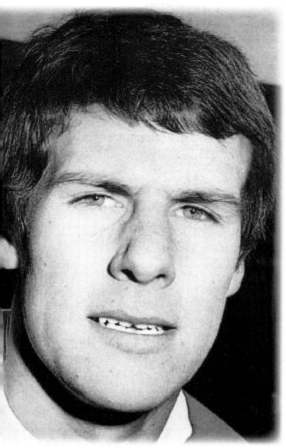

Blues were desperately short of goalscoring talent. Royle was one of the most prolific goalscorers since the war, scoring 119 goals in 272 games for Everton. He also won six international caps, the first coming against Malta in 1971.

He scored 31 goals in 117 games for the Maine Road club before moving on to Bristol City and later Norwich City where his playing career came to a premature end because of injury. Entering management with Oldham Athletic, he combined integrity, humour and sound judgement as the Latics won promotion from the Second Division and reached the League Cup Final and FA Cup semi-final.

In November 1994 he returned to Goodison as manager and though he kept the club in the Premiership, there were clashes with chairman Peter Johnson over transfer deals and these resulted in Royle leaving the club by mutual consent. Royle, who talks eagerly about the game and the people in it, took Manchester City into the Premiership after successive promotions but lost his job following the club's relegation at the end of the 2000-01 season.

Royle was the Blues' leading marksman in the 1968-69 season with 22 goals and again the following season with 23 goals as Everton won the League Championship. He was one of the deadliest strikers of a ball in the First Division. He was powerful with a clinical finish and an ability to head the ball, not seen at Goodison since the days of Dixie Dean. His career, however, was dogged by injury and he eventually moved to Manchester City. Nevertheless it was a little surprising that Everton boss Billy Bingham should let him go at the time he did, for the

Honours
League Championship
1969-70
6 England caps

TED SAGAR

Born	7 February 1910
Birthplace	Campsall
Height	5ft 10ins
Weight	10st 10lbs

Team	Apps	Gls
Everton	463	0

Everton legend Ted Sagar was one of the finest goalkeepers of all-time. Yet except for a lack of foresight on the part of Hull City, he would possibly have never found his way to Goodison Park. As a youngster, he was playing for Thorne Colliery in the Doncaster Senior League when he was spotted by a Tigers' scout. The Boothferry Park club gave him a trial but were then slow to offer him a contract, allowing Everton to nip in and sign him from under their noses.

Sagar made his Football League debut for the Blues in a 4-0 home win over Derby County in January 1930, going on to make eight appearances during the course of that 1929-30 season. However, he did not make a single league appearance the following season, when Bill Coggins

" Combining sheer athleticism with tremendous vision and bravery, Sagar was famous for launching himself headlong at the ball, regardless of the number of players blocking his path."

was first choice, but was back in the side the next year when the club won the League Championship. Missing just one game, Sagar was in outstanding form as Dixie Dean netted 45 goals in 38 games.

In 1933 Sagar won an FA Cup winners' medal as the Blues beat Manchester City 3-0 in the Wembley final. It was the first time that players in a final had been numbered with Everton wearing 1 to 11 and City numbered 12 through to 22. City would have taken the lead after just fifteen seconds had Sagar not done well and held on to the ball when Toseland had flung over a high-searching far-post cross which dipped late. Although hardly overworked, Sagar's calm assurance when he handled the ball had c

noticeable effect on his team-mates. His confidence soon spread through the ranks and before long the Blues were in complete control.

Slim and perhaps even underweight for a goalkeeper in the days when it was legitimate for centre-forwards to bounce both keeper and ball into the back of the net, Sagar survived by skill alone. He had the uncanny ability to judge the high flight of a ball from the wings and was completely without nerves. Combining sheer athleticism with tremendous vision and bravery, he was famous for launching himself headlong at the ball, regardless of the number of players blocking his path.

He won his first England cap against Northern Ireland in October 1935 and was honoured on three further occasions against Scotland, Austria and Belgium.

He won another League Championship medal in 1938-39, a season during which he kept 18 clean sheets in 41 games. The only match he missed resulted in a 7-0 defeat for the Blues at the hands of Wolverhampton Wanderers.

When Sagar returned from war service with the Fifth Divisional Signals in Italy, he found George Bennett filling his position in the League side but he again proved his worth in the reserves and was able to regain his place in the League side.

When Sagar finally decided to retire in May 1953, he had established a club record for peacetime Football League appearances with a total of 463. This was a relatively low figure as his career spanned the war years and did not include the regional games in which he had played between 1939 and 1946.

Honours
League Championship
1931-32, 1938-39
FA Cup 1932-33
4 England caps

GRAEME SHARP

Born	16 October 1960	
Birthplace	Glasgow	
Height	6ft 1ins	
Weight	11st 8lbs	

Team	Apps	Gls
Everton	306 (16)	111
Oldham Ath.	103 (4)	30

G raeme Sharp was a virtual unknown when Blues' manager Gordon Lee splashed out £120,000 to bring the striker to Goodison Park from Dunfermline Athletic in April 1980. After making his debut as a substitute at Brighton the following month, he became unsettled and was slow to break into a struggling team, so much so that he even considered moving on. However, following the appointment of Howard Kendall his career began to blossom and he enjoyed a series of fruitful combinations, first with Adrian Heath, then Andy Gray and finally Gary Lineker.

It was Sharp who scored the Blues' opening goal in the 1984 FA Cup Final victory over Watford, while the following season he headed the equaliser against Bayern Munich in the European Cup Winners' Cup semi-final. In 1984-85, Sharp scored 30 goals in all competitions, the most spectacular and satisfying of all his strikes coming in that season's Merseyside derby at Anfield. Gary Stevens sent a long, high pass out of defence that droppe invitingly into the path of the centre forward; he took it down on his instep completely wrong-footing Mar Lawrenson in the process and as th ball sat up for him, he hit a dippin right-foot volley from fully 25 yarc that beat Grobbelaar's picturesqu leap all ends up! The net bulged an Everton had won 1-0.

The pinnacle of Sharp's meteoric ris to stardom came when Jock Stein gav him his first full Scottish outing in th World Cup qualifier against Iceland i May 1985. Not surprisingly his valu increased enormously and he was hig on the wanted lists of several leadin Italian clubs. When Ian Rush joine Juventus in 1987, he was asked whic player in the world he would like a a strike partner; the former Liverpoo and Wales forward had no hesitatio in naming Graeme Sharp.

As well as netting his own quot of goals, Graeme Sharp was a extremely unselfish provider whos positional sense was remarkabl acute. The Scotsman was an aeric playmaker who combined deftness and power with the ability to distribute as accurately with his head as most contemporaries could with their feet.

There is no doubt that Gary Lineker owes Sharp the greatest debt, for in 1985-86, when the Blues were runners-up in the League and the FA Cup, the former Leicester striker scored 38 goals, most of which the big Scot had a hand in.

After injuries restricted his appearances towards the end of Everton's League Championship winning season of 1986-87, Sharp's goal tally began to deteriorate. However, he still holds the record as the Blues' top post-war goalscorer and when it was announced that he was joining Oldham Athletic for £500,000 in July 1991 many Everton fans reckoned he was being released far too soon.

When Oldham manager Joe Royle returned to Goodison Park, Sharp became the Latics' manager but resigned his post in February 1997. The Scotsman is now a pundit for local radio.

Honours
League Championship
1984-85, 1986-87
FA Cup 1983-84
European Cup Winners' Cup
1984-85
12 Scotland caps

KEVIN SHEEDY

Born	21 October 1959
Birthplace	Builth Wells
Height	5ft 9ins
Weight	11st 5lbs

Team	Apps	Gls
Hereford Utd	47 (4)	4
Liverpool	1 (2)	0
Everton	263 (11)	67
Newcastle U	36 (1)	4
Blackpool	25 (1)	1

Kevin Sheedy began his Football League career with Hereford United before an £80,000 move to Liverpool in July 1978. However, things didn't work out for the young midfielder. In four years at Anfield he made just three League appearances for the Reds. He won four Central League Championship medals before he was rescued from obscurity in June 1982 when Everton manager Howard Kendall paid £100,000 for his services. Sheedy was anxious to move to a club where he could be assured of first-team football and after making his debut at Watford on the opening day of the 1982-83 season and having a hand in all of Everton's goals in a 5-0 rout of Aston Villa, he scored his first goal for the club in a 3-1 defeat of Spurs.

Sheedy made his international debut in October 1983 as a substitute in the game against Holland. Despite being born in mid-Wales, he had qualified to play for the Republic of Ireland through his father who was born in County Clare. His appearances were limited by injury as they were for Everton. He had no problem in securing himself a regular first team spot at Goodison yet he was still dogged by misfortune. He missed Everton's 2-0 win over Watford in the 1984 FA Cup Final through injury, thus missing out on a winners' medal.

Sheedy was back the following season, playing a vital role as Everton lifted the League Championship for the first time in fifteen years. He also scored the Blues' third goal in the European Cup Winners' Cup Final victory over Rapid Vienna.

Arguably one of the best midfielders of the 1980s, Sheedy was famed for his 'cultured' left foot, from which he combined accurate passing with deadly shooting either from free-kicks or open play. He scored some goals of superb quality - against Ipswich Town in the sixth round of the 1984-85 FA Cup he scored twice from a retaken free-kick. He bent the first attempt over the wall and into the net on

Paul Cooper's right but the referee hadn't blown for it to be taken. When the kick was re-taken he bent it over the wall again to Cooper's left!

In 1986-87, Sheedy was fully fit and helped Everton to win another League Championship title. The following year he was instrumental in his adopted country reaching the European Championship Finals and in 1990 he scored the Republic's first goal in a World Cup Finals when he equalised against England at Cagliari.

Towards the end of his career at Everton, Sheedy found it difficult to hold down his place in the side through injuries and inconsistent form. Giving up the chance of a testimonial, he moved to Newcastle United on a free transfer and in 1992-93 won a First Division Championship medal. He later played for Blackpool before becoming youth team manager at Blackburn Rovers.

Sheedy was assistant manager to his former Republic of Ireland colleague John Aldridge at Tranmere Rovers before taking over the reins on a temporary basis following Aldridge's resignation.

Honours
League Championship
1984-85, 1986-87
European Cup Winners' Cup
1984-85
47 Republic of Ireland caps

NEVILLE
SOUTHALL

Born	16 September 1958
Birthplace	Llandudno
Height	6ft 1ins
Weight	14st 0bs

Team	Apps	Gls
Bury	39	0
Everton	578	0
Port Vale (L)	9	0
Southend Utd (L)	9	0
Stoke City	12	0
Torquay Utd	53	0
Bradford City	1	0

As a boy, Neville Southall played for the Caernarvon District side as a centre-half but after limited success he shelved any thought about being an outfield player to concentrate on goalkeeping. He spent the six years between leaving school and becoming a full-time footballer working as a dustman, a cleaner and a hod carrier.

While living in Llandudno, Southall played for both Bangor City and Conwy United but it was his fine form at Winsford United that made Bury pay £9,000 for him in 1980. In the summer of 1981 and after only 44 first team appearances for the Shakers, he signed for Everton for £150,000.

After making his debut in a 2-1 win over Ipswich Town, things didn't go too smoothly for Southall and after a 5-0 home defeat at the hands of Liverpool he was dropped and sent on loan to Fourth Division Port Vale in January 1983. He returned to Goodison Park after nine games and was ever-present for that and the next two seasons as his form and Everton's improved beyond all expectation.

The Welshman made his international debut on 27 May 1982, keeping a clean sheet as Wales beat Northern Ireland 3-0. Along with Arsenal's Jack Kelsey, he is the finest goalkeeper to have represented Wales.

Southall's anticipation was superb and he was a good shot-stopper. Always displaying great courage, he was not afraid to dive in amid a mass of boots to take low crosses.

In 1984 he got his first taste of glory with Everton when the Blues won the FA Cup, beating Watford 2-0. The following season Everton won the League Championship, the European Cup Winners' Cup and reached the FA Cup Final. At the end of the season he became the fourth goalkeeper to win the Player of the Year award following in the footsteps of Ber

Trautmann, Gordon Banks and Pat Jennings - his years of hard work and dedication had paid off.

He suffered such a severe dislocation of the ankle and ligament damage playing for Wales against the Republic of Ireland in March 1986 that it was wondered if he would ever be able to get back to his brilliant best. However, he recovered in time to collect his second League Championship winners' medal in 1986-87.

Southall's part in one bizarre incident - a goalmouth sit-in after walking out of a half-time harangue by Everton manager Colin Harvey - did the big Welshman no credit, even though Southall is his own man and was acting out of frustration rather than malice.

There is no doubt that Southall's world-class performances played a major part in Everton's run to be one of England's top clubs. Though he possessed brilliant reflexes which enabled him to make some outstanding saves, what gave him the edge was an astonishing capacity to change direction at the last moment, sometimes even in mid-air.

On leaving Goodison, he joined Stoke City before playing for Torquay United and making a Premiership appearance for Bradford City. He was capped 92 times by Wales and his team-mate and former Liverpool centre-forward Ian Rush said, 'For sheer consistency, there's no-one to touch Neville Southall.'

Honours
League Championship
1984-85, 1986-87
FA Cup 1983-84
European Cup Winners' Cup
1984-85
92 Wales caps

TREVOR STEVEN

Born	21 September 1963
Birthplace	Berwick
Height	5ft 10ins
Weight	11st 7bs

Team	Apps	Gls
Burnley	74 (2)	11
Everton	210 (4)	48

Although he was educated at a rugby-playing school, Trevor Steven went on to achieve the unique feat of winning League Championship medals in three different countries! He began his Football League career with Burnley where he earned rave reviews game after game and the mature football brain in one so young soon had the bigger clubs tracking his progress. Still only 18, he was selected for the England youth squad for a European tournament and won his first international honour against Scotland at Highfield Road in March 1982.

In the summer of 1983 major changes were in the air at Turf Moor and within a week of the arrival of new manager John Bond, Trevor Steven was on his way to Everton for £325,000. On his arrival at Goodison he seemed a little over anxious to impress and understandably his form suffered. But by the start of the 1984-85 season he was back to his best, using his pace and deft footwork to leave opponents stranded before unleashing a thundering shot. He was also a great crosser of the ball and laid on Andy Gray's 1984 FA Cup Final clincher. Yet despite all these eye-catching skills, he possessed great stamina and versatility. Though he was at his best on the right, he was effective on either flank and in the first leg of the 1985 European Cup Winners' Cup semi-final against Bayern Munich stepped in to fill the breach as a striker because of injuries.

By now Steven was a full international, winning his first England cap in the World Cup qualifier against Northern Ireland in Belfast in February 1985. In 1986 Everton finished runners-up to Liverpool in both First Division and FA Cup. That summer he went with England to the World Cup in Mexico and played in the final stages of his country's campaign. When Everton won the League Championship in 1986-87, Steven top-scored with 14 goals, though his total included ten penalties.

In 1989 Everton reached the FA Cup Final once more, only to be beaten yet again by Liverpool at Wembley.

That final was to be Trevor Steven's last match in an Everton shirt, for once he had made it clear that he was Ibrox bound, Colin Harvey, Everton's manager, asked a British record fee of £2.5 million. A tribunal decided that a much fairer figure would be almost a million less and so in June 1989, Steven was transferred to Glasgow Rangers for £1.5 million. Rangers won the Scottish Premier League in 1990 and 1991.

In August 1991, as the new season was in its infancy, Steven was suddenly sold to French club Olympique Marseille for a colossal £5.5 million. At the end of his only season on the Riviera, Marseille won the French Championship before selling him back to Rangers for £2.4 million.

More Scottish Premier League Championship and League Cup winners' medals followed in 1993 and 1994. The Scottish Premier League title was secured again in 1995 and 1996 but Steven's contribution was only modest and soon he retired from the game.

Honours
League Championship
1984-85, 1986-87
FA Cup 1983-84
European Cup Winners' Cup
1984-85
32 England caps

GARY STEVENS

Born	27 March 1963	
Birthplace	Barrow	
Height	5ft 11ins	
Weight	12st 7bs	

Team	Apps	Gls
Everton	207 (1)	8
Tranmere R	126 (1)	2

Gary Stevens, who had been converted from midfielder to right-back as he rose through the Goodison youth system, made his first team debut in a 1-1 draw at West Ham United in October 1981. What let him down at this stage of his career was his work on the ball, especially his service to the forwards, which tended not only to be wayward but almost entirely of the aerial kind. However he returned to the club's Central League side and practised hard, eventually taking over from Brian Borrows in November 1982.

Stevens' form was a revelation with his natural sprinting ability and great composure on the ball led to him being called into Bobby Robson's England squad for the World Cup qualifier against Northern Ireland in February 1985. He made his full international debut in Mexico later that year against World Cup holders Italy.

Having won an FA Cup winners' medal in 1984 and a League Championship medal in 1985, Stevens was a member of the Everton side that won the European Cup Winners' Cup that same year, beating Rapid Vienna 3-1 in the final in Rotterdam. Along with Lineker, Reid and Steven, he was one of the Everton quartet in England's team which reached the 1986 World Cup quarter-finals but then he suffered an injury that forced him to miss much of the first-half of the club's League Championship winning season of 1986-87.

Possessing one of the game's longest throws, he became increasingly effective in attack as his all-round expertise developed. Though he wasn't often on the scoresheet, one of his most memorable goals came in the third round League Cup tie against Liverpool at Anfield in October 1987 when his 20-yard deflected left-footer proved to be the only goal of the game.

However, during the course of that 1987-88 season, Stevens not only

medals, a Scottish Cup winners' medal and three Scottish League Cup medals.

In September 1994, after making 245 appearances for the Scottish giants, he returned to Merseyside to play for Tranmere Rovers, costing the Prenton Park club £350,000.

Gary Stevens' versatility and experience proved an invaluable asset in is four seasons on the Wirral where, apart from a spell when he suffered a badly broken forearm, he missed very few games. He appeared in 150 League and Cup games

suffered from a series of niggling injuries but also had his differences with manager Colin Harvey and it came as no surprise when in the summer of 1988 he left Goodison to join Glasgow Rangers for £1.25 million. Consequently, his move to Ibrox, where he was to excel, turned out to be in the best interests of all concerned. With Rangers he won six Scottish Premier Division Championship

for Rovers before being released in the summer of 1998, after which he decided to retire.

Honours
League Championship
1984-85, 1986-87
FA Cup 1983-84
European Cup Winners' Cup
1984-85
46 England caps

DEREK TEMPLE

Born	13 November 1938	
Birthplace	Liverpool	
Height	5ft 8ins	
Weight	11st 4lbs	

Team	Apps	Gls
Everton	231 (1)	72
Preston NE	75 (1)	14

Scoring the winning goal in the 1966 FA Cup Final against Sheffield Wednesday has guaranteed Derek Temple a place in Everton's 'Hall of Fame'. As a free-scoring schoolboy, playing for both Lancashire and England, Temple had been a target for both Everton and Liverpool. Shortly after leaving school, he threw in his lot with the Blues where his form with the Colts was astonishing. In one season alone he scored 70 goals, routinely scoring five or six a match.

"Temple was adept at timing his arrival in the penalty area to capitalise on long crosses"

Temple made a promising senior start in the spring of 1957 as the Blues beat Newcastle United 2-1. He kept his place for the remaining seven games of the campaign, scoring three goals, including one in his second game in a 2-2 draw at Sheffield Wednesday. The following season he consolidated, moving to inside-forward and linking well with Dave Hickson. The highlight of Temple's season was his double-strike in a 3-3 home draw with Manchester United but his progress was then hampered by two years of National Service.

On his return from East Africa where he had been used to playing at an altitude of 7,000 feet, Temple struggled to come to terms with top flight football and there was talk of a transfer. Thankfully that didn't happen and he worked hard to build up his strength and fitness. After the Blues' new manager Harry Catterick switched him to the wing he found himself back in the limelight.

In 1961-62, Temple netted 10 times in 17 outings, including a well-taken hat-trick in a 5-2 home win against Ipswich Town. He seemed set to win a regular place in the Everton side the following term but was sidelined by a knee injury that needed a cartilage

Adept at timing his arrival in the penalty area to capitalise on long crosses from Alex Scott, one of Temple's most spectacular goals came in the club's run to the 1966 FA Cup Final. When the Blues beat Manchester City 2-0 in the quarter-final second replay at Molineux, Temple crashed home the second goal with a shoulder-high left-foot volley. Of course his most important goal was that winner in the 1966 FA Cup Final. As the ball squirmed under Gerry Young's boot, Temple pounced, carrying the ball unchallenged before arrowing an inch-perfect drive past Ron Springett's right-hand into the corner of the net.

operation and consequently he missed out on a League Championship medal.

A utility man who could fill a variety of roles, Temple came into his own in 1963-64, usually appearing on the left-wing. Later he moved to inside-left to accommodate Johnny Morrissey but he was rarely absent from the side for the next four seasons. He was skilful with both feet and could create opportunities out of nothing. His talents were recognised by England manager Alf Ramsey, who awarded him his sole cap against West Germany in Nuremberg in 1965.

Not always a favourite with the Goodison crowd, he later lost confidence and in September 1967 he was transferred to Preston North End. Three years later he joined Wigan Athletic. On leaving the game he worked in the glass industry and he is now in charge of the Merseyside branch of an industrial cleaning company.

Honours
FA Cup 1965-66
1 England cap

DAVID UNSWORTH

Born	16 October 1973
Birthplace	Chorley
Height	6ft 1ins
Weight	14st 2lbs

Team	Apps	Gls
Everton	240 (28)	31
West Ham	32	2

David Unsworth made his Football League debut for Everton while still a trainee, at Tottenham Hotspur in April 1992. Although substituting at left-back for the injured Andy Hinchcliffe, he scored a stunning equalising goal for the Blues with a first touch volley from a corner in a 3-3 thriller. In his early days at Goodison, many Everton fans thought the club had unearthed the natural long-term successor to Welsh international Kevin Ratcliffe. Like the former skipper, Unsworth was a quick, powerfully efficient left-sided central defender though he had started his career as a left-back.

It was Mike Walker who switched Unsworth to the centre of defence and he responded by making a tremendous impression during the 1994-95 season. He gave a majestic Merseyside derby performance in November as the Blues beat Liverpool 2-0, followed by a succession of dominant displays in the FA Cup. In the final, Everton beat Manchester United 1-0 with Unsworth playing alongside Dave Watson, completely muzzling the formidable Mark Hughes.

England manager Terry Venables called him up for the national squad and he made his full international debut in the 2-1 win over Japan in June 1995 but unfortunately he has since failed to add to his collection. Not surprisingly, he was voted Everton's 'Player of the Season'.

At the start of the 1995-96 season, he seemed strangely hesitant and there followed a sequence of indifferent form, though he was usually in the team. It was only towards the end of the following season that Unsworth showed signs of rediscovering the form that won him his solitary England cap. His composure in front of goal was outstanding for a defender and, as well as slotting home some high pressure penalties, he scored several times from open play.

Much to the consternation of many

After transferring the claret and blue of West Ham for Aston Villa, he soon realised that his former employers, Everton, also coveted his signature. After pleading with the Villa hierarchy he was allowed to join the Blues for the same £3 million fee Villa had paid the Hammers, without kicking a ball! He soon settled comfortably back into life at Goodison Park, immediately displaying the defensive assurance and strength which had endeared him to Hammers' fans.

Appointed club captain, Unsworth has best been employed on the left of a three-man defence, a role to which he has applied himself diligently and enthusiastically. One of the club's most consistent payers of recent years, he remains one of the Premiership's most solid and reliable defenders.

Everton supporters, Unsworth left Goodison in the summer of 1997, joining West Ham United for a fee of £1 million with the Hammers' midfielder Danny Williamson moving in the opposite direction. Despite having an excellent season at Upton Park, there was talk of him being unsettled in the south and in the summer of 1998 he was involved in one of the most bizarre transfers in Premiership history.

Honours
FA Cup 1994-95
1 England cap

ROY VERNON

Born	14 April 1937	
Birthplace	Prestatyn	
Height	5ft 11ins	
Weight	11st 10lbs	

Team	Apps	Gls
Blackburn R	131	49
Everton	176	101
Stoke City	84 (3)	22
Halifax Town	4	0

Roy Vernon had the chance to come to Goodison Park as a schoolboy but he turned down the opportunity and joined Blackburn Rovers groundstaff where he developed under the watchful eye of Blackburn manager Johnny Carey. Within twelve months of making his League debut for the Ewood Park club in September 1955, Vernon was a regular member of the Rovers side, displaying a maturity far beyond his years.

Vernon was a creative player who struck a dead ball with tremendous power. Dark, lean and lithe, he had great acceleration and was the deadliest of finishers. He graduated to the Welsh squad in time to be involved in the 1958 World Cup.

When Johnny Carey left Blackburn to manage Everton, Vernon began to clash with the new Rovers manager Dally Duncan. Meanwhile at Goodison, the search was on to find a centre-forward who could link up with the diminutive Scot Bobby Collins. There were a number around but they were of course, expensive. However, with Blues' Chairman John Moores encouraging the club to be more extravagant, the possibilities opened up. Top of the list was Roy Vernon, so in February 1960, he followed his mentor to Goodison Park in a £27,000 deal which took Eddie Thomas to Blackburn in part-exchange. Vernon made his Everton debut in a 2-0 home defeat at the hands of Wolverhampton Wanderers, going on to score nine goals in the last twelve games of the season.

"Vernon was the architect of Everton's Championship victory of 1962-63. In the final game Everton needed to beat Fulham to clinch the title - Roy hit a magnificent hat-trick in a 4-1 win to finish the season with 24 league goals."

In 1960-61, his first full season with the Toffees, he was magnificent. He knocked in 21 goals, including a hat-trick in a 4-1 win over Arsenal on the final day of the season. He was top scorer again the following season, after Collins' departure to Leeds, with 26 goals, striking up a good understanding with the newly-arrived Alex Young. Included in that total was another hat-trick in an 8-3 home win over Cardiff City.

Vernon was the architect of Everton's Championship victory of 1962-63. As the last game of the season approached, Everton needed to beat Fulham at home to clinch the title. He hit a magnificent hat-trick in a 4-1 win and finished the season with 24 league goals. He top-scored again in 1963-64 and had by now developed into one of the finest creative players of the early 1960s. There were occasional brushes with Carey's successor Harry Catterick, who made Vernon captain in the hope that the responsibility would mellow and mature the tempestuous Welshman. The arrival of Fred Pickering heralded the departure of Vernon in March 1965 to Stoke City for £40,000.

During his six seasons with the Blues, Vernon was as dangerous as any striker in the First Division at that time, scoring 110 goals in 199 League and Cup games. He later had a brief spell with Halifax Town and spent some time playing in South Africa before returning to the north-west to play alongside former Blackburn team-mates Ronnie Clayton and Bryan Douglas at Great Harwood.

Honours
League Championship
1962-63
32 Wales caps

DAVE WATSON

Born	20 November 1960
Birthplace	Liverpool
Height	6ft 0ins
Weight	12st 4lbs

Team	Apps	Gls
Norwich City	212	11
Everton	419 (4)	23

Dave Watson began his career with Liverpool, but after failing to reach the first team he moved to Norwich City in November 1980. The Canaries paid an initial fee of £50,000, a similar sum after Watson had made 25 senior appearances and a further £100,000 after he had collected his first full England cap.

In the summer of 1986, while Everton were preparing for the new season with a series of friendly games in Holland, manager Howard Kendall was informed that centre-half Derek Mountfield would be out of action for a number of weeks through injury. The Blues' manager was determined to start the campaign with a fully fit complement of senior players and so contacted Norwich boss Ken Brown to ask about the availability of Watson. In so doing, he started a ten-day tug-of-war in which his initial advances were spurned by the Carrow Road club until he raised his bid to a club record £900,000.

Initially, Watson appeared indecisive and clumsy and was caught out of position far too often. He constantly found himself at odds with supporters on the Gwladys Street terraces who idolised Mountfield, the man he had replaced. In fact, at one stage in the autumn of 1986, he was dropped in favour of the fit again Mountfield but as the season began to unfold, he came to terms with the Blues' zonal marking system and helped the club lift the League Championship.

Having won a place in the hearts of the Everton faithful with his raw courage and never-say-die attitude, Watson was voted the club's Player of the Year in 1987-88.

In 1991, Peter Reid, then manager of Manchester City, offered £1 million to take his former team-mate to Maine Road. Happily for Everton, Watson put his name to a new contract and was soon handed the job of skipper. He had by now become much more positive in attack, acquiring the welcome knack of chipping in with priceless goals.

In February 1991 Watson scored a fifth round FA Cup second replay winner against Liverpool and a subsequent quarter-final strike against West Ham United. Perhaps even more memorable was his header that won the 1995 quarter-final against Newcastle United. The Blues went on to win that season's FA Cup with Watson being named Man-of-the-Match in a 1-0 win over Manchester United.

Watson, who had seen defensive partners come and go, stepped up to become caretaker-manager after Joe Royle's departure and steered the club safely through a relegation dogfight in the spring of 1997. He then began to suffer with back and knee problems and shortly after his 36th birthday, he needed a cartilage operation. Though he lost the captaincy to Gary Speed, this most inspirational of players was recalled to the side by Walter Smith for the 1998-99 season, ending the campaign with the captain's armband back in his possession.

Though he finally began to show signs of wear and tear, such was the esteem in which Dave Watson was held at Goodison that his playing contract was extended. Finally he ended his Everton career just three matches short of the outfield appearance record at the club held by Brian Labone. Though a considerable influence in a coaching capacity, Dave Watson finally severed his links with the Blues, crossing the Mersey to manage Tranmere Rovers.

Honours
League Championship
1986-87
FA Cup 1994-95
12 England caps

GORDON WEST

Born	24 April 1943
Birthplace	Darfield
Height	6ft 11ins
Weight	14st 0lbs

Team	Apps	Gls
Blackpool	31	0
Everton	335	0
Tranmere R	17	0

Though he had trials with several clubs as a schoolboy centre-half, Gordon West was born to keep goal. He made his First Division debut for Blackpool as a 17-year-old, temporarily replacing Tony Waiters in the Seasiders' goal. His performances for the Bloomfield Road club led to Blues' manager Harry Catterick handing over £27,000, then a record fee for a keeper, to make his first signing as Everton boss. It was certainly a bold move but one that paid dividends for in 1962-63, his first full season, West replaced Albert Dunlop and helped the Blues win the League Championship, keeping 17 clean sheets in 38 appearances.

However, over the next couple of seasons, West shared the goalkeeping duties with the ever-improving Andy Rankin before re-asserting himself on the club's 1966 Wembley trail. In the seven matches on the way to the final, West didn't concede a goal and was outstanding in the games against Coventry and Manchester City.

Though he was one of the most flamboyant characters of the Catterick era, the dressing-room joker, he was also notoriously nervous prior to a game. He enjoyed a particularly warm relationship with Liverpool fans, to whom he endeared himself by blowing them a kiss after a torrent of abuse. The Kop's response was to present him with a handbag!

West's humour also shone through in the game against Newcastle United in October 1967, a match the Blues lost 1-0. The Everton keeper had been sent off for punching the Magpies' forward Albert Bennett and was replaced between the posts by Sandy Brown. At the final whistle, West had his team-mates in stitches as he berated poor Sandy for failing to save the resultant penalty!

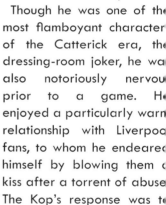

Finils in Mexico, preferring instead to remain at home with his family.

In 1970-71, West fell out of favour but again confounded the doubters by returning to be ever-present the following season. However, after David Lawson arrived from Huddersfield Town, West made only four more League appearances before deciding to retire. Two years later, he was lured back to the game by Tranmere Rovers. After shedding some weight he provided the Prenton Park club with four seasons of first-team cover. After working on the groundstaff at the Wirral-based club, he went to work in security on Merseyside.

Though he never quite scaled the heights predicted for him, Gordon West was without doubt one of the First Division's leading keepers throughout the

Following Everton's FA Cup win, West missed very few games over the following four seasons, picking up a second League Championship medal in 1969-70. His consistency brought him to the attention of Sir Alf Ramsey but West staggered the football world when he refused to join the England party for the 1970 World Cup sixties. In fact, it wasn't until the arrival of Neville Southall that the Blues were to find a truly satisfactory replacement.

Honours
League Championship
1962-63, 1969-70
FA Cup 1965-66
3 England caps

RAY WILSON

Born	17 December 1934	
Birthplace	Shirebrook	
Height	5ft 8ins	
Weight	11st 6lbs	

Team	Apps	Gls
Huddersfield T	266 (6)	6
Everton	114 (2)	0
Oldham Ath.	25	0
Bradford City	2	0

Ray Wilson had no burning ambition to be a professional footballer but he did play for his local youth club in the Derbyshire mining village of Shirebrook. One day the youth club had no game and Ray was asked to turn out for an open-age side and scored all his team's goals in a 6-3 defeat. He was asked to go for a trial with Huddersfield Town and they immediately offered him terms as an apprentice professional. At Leeds Road he came under the expert eye of coach Ray Goodall, who with Sam Wadsworth had formed the legendary full-back partnership of the Huddersfield side that won the League Championship in three successive seasons between 1924 and 1926.

When he returned from National Service in 1955, Wilson was still playing at inside-left; it was Goodall who switched him with great success to full-back. He made his League debut for Town in October 1955 against Manchester United in a First Division match. He played in six games that season as the Yorkshire club were relegated to the Second Division.

Wilson arrived at Goodison in June 1964 in a £50,000 deal that took Mick Meagan in the opposite direction. He was now 29 and already had 266 League games under his belt with Huddersfield. He had already played 30 times for England and was regarded as the best left-back in Europe.

Not only did he help the Blues win the FA Cup at Sheffield Wednesday's expense but Wilson was to return to Wembley within a matter of months to play his part in England's sensational World Cup triumph. He was the only Everton player in Alf Ramsey's victorious side - Alan Ball was still with Blackpool at that time. He went on to play in the 1968 FA Cup Final as Everton lost to West Bromwich Albion, Jeff Astle scoring the only goal of the game.

A competent defender, Wilson was composed and looked in command even in the most difficult of situations. He always played to his strengths and if he did have a weakness, it was his

heading. Ray will never forget his headed clearance that gifted Haller the opening goal of the 1966 World Cup Final. From that moment on though, he never put a foot wrong. He won 63 caps for England, a record for a full-back for almost twenty years until it was surpassed by Kenny Sansom.

In May 1969, Wilson was given a free transfer. He had twisted his knee at the start of the 1968-69 campaign and though he tried to come back as the season progressed, it never felt right and he had to call it a day at

Goodison. He was a great influence in the four years he was at Everton and if he'd joined the club ten years earlier than he did, he would have been one of the all-time greats. After a brief spell with Oldham Athletic, he became player-coach of Bradford City.

One of the finest left-backs in footballing history, Wilson built up a successful career as an undertaker when he finally retired from the game.

Honours
FA Cup 1965-66
63 England caps

TOMMY WRIGHT

Born	21 October 1944
Birthplace	Liverpool
Height	5ft 9ins
Weight	11st 3lbs

Team	Apps	Gls
Everton	307 (1)	4

The classic case of a local boy made good, Tommy Wright joined Everton straight from school as a talented inside-forward. In the early 1960s, he was a member of the Blues' 'A' side, playing in midfield alongside John Hurst and Colin Harvey. Unfortunately he was not making the progress required of him and it was only after injuries prompted a reshuffle and he found himself at right-back that he began to impress. By the middle of the 1964-65 season, Wright had joined the club's senior ranks as the long-term replacement for the strong-tackling Alex Parker.

Wright was a shrewd tactician who delighted his front men with his constructive passing and pin-point crosses from his forays down the flank. One of the Blues' most dangerous attacking moves involved winger Jimmy Husband cutting inside to leave a gap for the No.2 to charge into before picking out the head of Joe Royle. Though Wright enjoyed getting forward, such was his athleticism that he rarely got stranded upfield.

Having clawed back a two-goal deficit in the 1966 FA Cup Final against Sheffield Wednesday, the Blues had just taken the lead when Wright began to suffer with chronic cramp. With time running out, the Owls attacked down their left-flank, desperate for an equalising goal. The Blues' defence were at sixes and sevens and Wright was the only player in a position to give chase. Ignoring the obvious pain he was in he sprinted, made the interception and cleared with the minimum of fuss.

His form was such that after playing for England at Under-23 level, he won his first full international honours

two vital points in the match against Nottingham Forest.

Wright was still at his peak when, at the end of the 1972-73 season, aged only 29, he was forced into premature retirement following recurring knee trouble.

Along with fellow international Ray Wilson, he formed, without doubt, the best full-back pairing the Blues have ever had. Though the World Cup winner tended to get most of the limelight, Wright's all-round talent and superb temperament would have graced any leading First Division side of his era.

Tommy Wright, whose nephew Billy followed him into the Everton side towards the end of the decade, will always be remembered as one of football's natural gentlemen.

against Russia in the European Championships of 1968. He went on to represent his country in the 1970 World Cup Finals in Mexico where, in the match against Brazil, he had an outstanding game.

Despite taking a number of knocks, usually to his knees, Wright missed very few games and between 1966 and 1971 he was absent for only seven league games. When the Blues won the League Championship in 1969-70, Wright was one of four ever-presents, his only goal of the campaign securing

> *"Wright was a shrewd tactician who delighted his front men with his constructive passing and pin-point crosses from his forays down the flank."*

Honours
League Championship
1969-70
FA Cup 1965-66
11 England caps

ALEX YOUNG

Born	3 February 1937	
Birthplace	Loanhead	
Height	5ft 11ins	
Weight	11st 8lbs	

Team	Apps	Gls
Everton	227 (1)	77
Stockport Co.	23	5

Alex Young signed for Scottish club Hearts of Midlothian from Newtongrange Star and made his debut as an 18-year-old. In five seasons with the Tynecastle club, he scored 77 goals including 20 in the club's record-breaking 1957-58 Championship campaign and 23 when they recaptured the title in 1959-60.

He joined Everton in November 1960 in a £55,000 deal that brought team-mate and full-back George Thomson to Goodison and he soon won over the Blues' fans with his class. Young didn't make his Everton debut until the following month because he arrived on Merseyside carrying a nasty knee injury sustained in playing for the British Army. His debut didn't produce the best of results as Everton lost 3-1 to Spurs but for the rest of the season, Young and Roy Vernon began to blossom as a partnership and after he hit his first goals for the club - a double against Blackburn Rovers - there was no holding them. The Blues won six out of the last seven games of the season to finish fifth in the First Division.

In the Championship-winning season of 1962-63, Young scored in each of the opening three games, all victories. He ended the season with 22 goals including the only goal of the game against Tottenham Hotspur that took Everton to the top of the League - a position from which they were never dislodged.

Arguably the greatest Scottish player to sign for Everton and Young was a major influence on the side that beat Sheffield Wednesday 3-2 in the 1966 FA Cup Final.

In attacking situations, Young always seemed to have plenty of time. He knew where to play the ball instinctively - he didn't have to look where he was passing and was aware

"Young was one of the classiest players in post-war football and Everton fans worshipped him; to them he was the greatest!"

distinctive figure on the field and the fans called him the 'Golden Vision'. He was a gifted, elegant striker and when he was replaced by a 16-year-old youngster by the name of Joe Royle for a game at Blackpool near the end of his career, there was a public outcry. Manager Harry Catterick was assaulted by outraged Everton supporters - such was Young's popularity.

In August 1968, Young became player-manager of Glentoran. He only spent two months

of all the options open to him without looking up. For all his flair and grace, he possessed a vicious shot and had good heading ability.

Yet, despite his subtlety, skill and natural ability, he only played for Scotland on eight occasions, making his debut in a 1-1 draw against England in 1960 - he surely should have played many more times. Like many players with flair and genius, he set himself very high standards and was often very critical of his own game.

His blond hair made him quite a

across the sea before returning to join Stockport County. Sadly, he was forced to retire with knee trouble after just 23 games.

Young was one of the classiest players in post-war football and Everton fans worshipped him; to them he was the greatest!

Honours
League Championship
1962-63
FA Cup 1965-66
8 Scotland caps

The Merseyside Derby
League Results 1894 to 2002

Everton score first

Year	Goodison Pk	Anfield		Year	Goodison Pk	Anfield
1894-95	3-0	2-2		1950-51	1-3	2-0
1896-97	2-1	0-0		1962-63	2-2	0-0
1897-98	3-0	1-3		1963-64	3-1	1-2
1898-99	1-2	0-2		1964-65	2-1	4-0
1899-1900	3-2	2-1		1965-66	0-0	0-5
1900-01	1-1	2-1		1966-67	3-1	0-0
1901-02	4-0	2-2		1967-68	1-0	0-1
1902-03	3-1	0-0		1968-69	0-0	1-1
1903-04	5-2	2-2		1969-70	0-3	2-0
1905-06	4-2	1-1		1970-71	0-0	2-3
1906-07	0-0	2-1		1971-72	1-0	0-4
1907-08	2-4	0-0		1972-73	0-2	0-1
1908-09	5-0	1-0		1973-74	0-1	0-0
1909-10	2-3	1-0		1974-75	0-0	0-0
1910-11	0-1	2-0		1975-76	0-0	0-1
1911-12	2-1	3-1		1976-77	0-0	1-3
1912-13	0-2	2-0		1977-78	0-1	0-0
1913-14	1-2	2-1		1978-79	1-0	1-1
1914-15	1-3	5-0		1979-80	1-2	2-2
1919-20	0-0	1-3		1980-81	2-2	0-1
1920-21	0-3	0-1		1981-82	1-3	1-3
1921-22	1-1	1-1		1982-83	0-5	0-0
1922-23	0-1	1-5		1983-84	1-1	0-3
1923-24	1-0	2-1		1984-85	1-0	1-0
1924-25	0-1	1-3		1985-86	2-3	2-0
1925-26	3-3	1-5		1986-87	0-0	1-3
1926-27	1-0	0-1		1987-88	1-0	0-2
1927-28	1-1	3-3		1988-89	0-0	1-1
1928-29	1-0	2-1		1989-90	1-3	1-2
1929-30	3-3	3-0		1990-91	2-3	1-3
1931-32	2-1	3-1		1991-92	1-1	1-3
1932-33	3-1	4-7		1992-93	2-1	0-1
1933-34	0-0	2-3		1993-94	2-0	1-2
1934-35	1-0	1-2		1994-95	2-0	0-0
1935-36	0-0	0-6		1995-96	1-1	2-1
1936-37	2-0	2-3		1996-97	1-1	1-1
1937-38	1-3	2-1		1997-98	2-0	1-1
1938-39	2-1	3-0		1998-99	0-0	2-3
1946-47	1-0	0-0		1999-2000	0-0	1-0
1947-48	0-3	0-4		2000-01	2-3	1-3
1948-49	1-1	0-0		2001-02	1-3	1-1
1949-50	0-0	1-3		2002-03	1-2	0-0

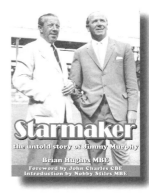
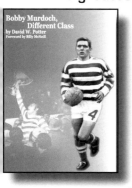
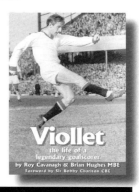

The King

Denis Law, Hero of the Stretford End
by Brian Hughes MBE
ISBN: 1901746356 - £17.95 - 421 pp
'The Greatest Thing on Two Feet'
BILL SHANKLY

Denis Law was hero and villain all rolled into one. His high-octane performances made him a Boys' Own hero to many. He was a player capable of incredible feats of skill and power - all carried off with the knowing smile and villainous touch of a Piccadilly pickpocket. To Mancunians, this son of an Aberdonian trawlerman became part of the fabric of the city; first as a dynamic frontman for the Blues and later as an all-action hero at Matt Busby's United.

In the latest of his biographies of former United greats, Brian Hughes traces the Scot's transformation from unlikely looking teenage footballer to the world's preeminent striker. Law's progress up the football ladder was prolific. The bespectacled youth who joined Huddersfield in 1955 didn't look much like a future world star but Bill Shankly's first reaction to his performances on the pitch were telling - 'he's terror', said the then Huddersfield boss.

But if Denis' subsequent transfers to Manchester City and later Torino confirmed his status as football's rising star, his arrival at Old Trafford in 1962 confirmed him as phenomenon. The Reds £115,000 swoop secured a player of huge influence both on and off the pitch. For 11 years his personality dominated the thoughts of United fans as Lawmania gripped the city until his shock transfer to the Blues in 1973.

Thus the stage was set for the ironic denouement in April 1974 - Denis' backheel consigning United to Second Division football and the Law legend to immortality.

'Out of the Void'
The Story of Primal Scream
by Brendan Yates
Published September 2003
ISBN: 1901746364 - £10.99 - 260pp

'From leather-clad rock icons to Ecstasy popping ravers, Primal Scream have appealed too and appalled their following in equal measure'

Goodison Maestros

The 50 Greatest Everton players since 1945

By Dean Hayes

EMPIRE
PUBLICATIONS

First published in 2003

EMPIRE PUBLICATIONS
1 Newton Street, Manchester M1 1HW
© Dean Hayes 2003

ISBN: 190174633X

Photographs courtesy of Liverpool Echo & Lancashire Evening Post
Jacket design & Layout: Ashley Shaw
Edited by Ashley Shaw & Stuart Fish